DORKING

A Surrey Market Town through Twenty Centuries

Contributing Authors
Vivien Ettlinger
Alan A Jackson
Brian Overell

Edited by Alan A. Jackson

DORKING LOCAL HISTORY GROUP

First published in 1991 by the Local History Group of the Dorking and District Preservation Society, Dorking Museum, West Street, Dorking, Surrey RH4 1BS.

ISBN 1 870912 03 9

Printed by Rayment Printers Ltd., 5 Horsham Road, Dorking, Surrey.

Cover illustration: Dorking High Street on Market Day, *Etching by Charles Collins, c. 1895, (Mary Day).*

CONTENTS

Page

What They Have Said About Dorking 5

Introduction 9

1. The Early Settlement and Manor
   Vivien Ettlinger 11

2. Medieval Manor and Market: 1300–1485
   Vivien Ettlinger 15

3. Tudor and Early Stuart Town: 1486–1642
   Vivien Ettlinger 23

4. Commonwealth and Restoration Dorking: 1643–1688
   Vivien Ettlinger 29

5. The Long Eighteenth Century: 1689–1836
   Brian Overell 37

6. Victorian Progress and Growth: 1837–1900
   Alan A Jackson 67

7. The Town in the Motor Age: 1901–1991
   Alan A Jackson 87

Appendix: Population Figures 109

Sources and Bibliography 110

Index 117

MAPS

Hypothetical Map of Dorking in the late Middle Ages 18

Dorking in 1594 22

Dorking in 1649 30

Dorking in 1780 41

Dorking in 1850 72

Dorking in 1914 89

Dorking in 1939 91

Dorking from the north-east. *Etching by Percy Robertson (1869–1934)*. *(Surrey Archaeological Society)*

WHAT THEY HAVE SAID ABOUT DORKING

I went to DARKING to see Mr. Charles Howard's Ampitheater Garden, or Solitarie recesse, being 15 Ackers [acres], invirond by an hill; he shew'd us divers rare plants; caves, and an Elaboratory. — John Evelyn's *Diary,* 1 August 1655 on a visit to Deepdene.

The town of Darking is eminent for several little things worth observation; as first, for the great Roman highway called Stonny-street, which Mr. Cambden says, passes through the very churchyard of this town. Secondly, for a little common or heath, called Cottman Dean . . . which some learned physicians have singled out for the best air in England. Thirdly for Mr. Howard's house and garden, called Deaden [Deepdene]. — Daniel Defoe, *A Tour Through The Whole Island of Britain,* 1724.

In the summer the town and its environs are usually thronged with company, and lodgings are in great request. — John Timbs, *A Picturesque Promenade Round Dorking in Surrey,* 1823.

Dorking is a remarkably clean and pleasant country town and has long been a favourite place of resort in the summer season . . . the whole neighbourhood is little else than a garden, too, of the most alluring and satisfying kind. Its walks and prospects are delightful . . . The Deepdene has long been celebrated as a place of considerable beauty. Aubrey even in his time calls it an Epitome of Paradise, and says he expects to see nothing like it except in the Kingdom of Heaven . . . . . — W. Thorne, *The Garden of Surrey or a Sketch of Dorking and of the Beautiful Country surrounding it,* 1829.

Dorking is indeed the very *beau ideal* of an English town, where comfort and beauty happily combine. — *Civil Service Gazette,* 1855.

The *Town* is well built, clean, has good shops, lies in a sheltered valley, and used to have a certain air of picturesque rusticity, but every year something more of this is worn off, and the town itself becomes less and less interesting to a stranger. It lies, however, in the midst of the most charming scenery of Surrey, is a good centre for its exploration, and possesses two excellent inns . . . — James Thorne, *Handbook to the Environs of London,* 1876.

Dorking is not a growing place, and it is not likely to become so while residence there is equivalent to complete isolation in the midst of beautiful scenery. Returned 'colonists' and others are apt to think that a town like Dorking is the very place to settle down in, but they make a great mistake. They, of all others, are the least fitted to stand the weary strain of the small and narrow tone and depressing social atmosphere of such a spot. After an active life in the busy world, a man who came to live in Dorking would perish miserably of utter boredom and dry rot . . . At Dorking, the tone of 'society' must be rather wearisome, for the landowners will not recognise the general residents, unless, indeed it be in that condescending manner which does not add much to the geniality of social intercourse. The town is therefore, at all seasons, one of the dullest in England; — and for young people it must be intolerable, for there is scarcely anybody of their own age to associate with them, there are no amusements, no one gives any parties, there are the usual narrow influences at work which always grow up in small gossipy places, and altogether life is stagnant there. — Louis J. Jennings, *Field Paths and Green Lanes,* 1877.

. . . for those who desire to live apart from their place of business; or have retired from the engagements of active life; or who are strangers from the metropolis or other places and seek pleasant scenery, salubrious air, and freedom from the excitement of a large population. — J. S. Bright on the new Holloway Estate in *A History of Dorking and The Neighbouring Parishes,* 1884.

The old-fashioned town of Dorking . . . is situated in a valley at the foot of the North Downs . . . and in the centre of as beautiful scenery of its kind as England can show . . . the town itself, though well built and thriving, contains little of interest except the church . . . — G. Phillips Bevan, *Tourists' Guide to the County of Surrey,* Third Edition, 1887.

It is evidence sufficient in itself to recommend our dear old town to the notice of those seeking a spot 'far from the madding crowd' where they can recruit their relapsed energies and reinvigorate their constitution while, at the same time their eyes may be gladdened and their hearts delighted with the beauties of nature of which the locality can proudly boast. — Editorial in *The Dorking Advertiser* on the Medical Officer of Health's Report for 1888.

I came back from Dorking on Monday night with an upright body, a clear eye, a fresh complexion and all the 'joy of living' pulsing in my veins. I had climbed the hills, I had breathed the air, I had looked upon the glorious landscape bathed in sunshine . . . Dorking for all its beauties, is not lively of an evening and if I were to get an extra special attack of 'le spleen' I should only have the Salvation Army Barracks to fall back upon for musical entertainment. But after all, one doesn't want much evening amusement at Dorking. The air is so strong that, after a day spent on the hills and in the valleys, one is very glad to go to bed . . . Soon after 10 o'clock, silence falls upon this little town and the lights go out, one by one. — George R. Sims in *The Referee,* April 1894.

Owing to its environment of considerable hills the climate of the town is rather relaxing in summer, so that visitors contemplating a prolonged sojourn should endeavour to get quarters in the southern outskirts, where there are many pleasant houses of various sizes on ground well above the valley. — C. S. Ward, *Surrey and Sussex,* Third Edition, 1905.

Dorking people want an earthquake to arouse them but when they are roused, they will keep going. — Canon Edward Arthur Chichester (1849–1925).

We do not want to turn Dorking into Stoneleigh . . . we are getting suburban enough as it is. — Miss F. M. Douglas JP, 1936 (during a council discussion on numbering houses distinguished only by names).

Dorking shows how the elements of character combine to produce an effect greater than the sum of the constituent parts; it is altogether an attractive Surrey town. — Anon, *Antiquities and Conservation Areas of Surrey,* Sixth Edition, 1976.

Dorking has long enjoyed a well deserved popularity with walkers . . . [it] has very good communications with both London and the villages along the Greensand Way . . . Add to all this some excellent restaurants and lots of pretty girls and it is little wonder that Dorking is worthy of a lengthy stay. — Jim Mc Lennan, *The Greensand Way, an Illustrated Guide,* 1984.

INTRODUCTION

'Dorking is, for the most part, without historical associations, and devoid of noticeable antiquities'

So wrote John Dennis in his *Handbook of Dorking* published in 1855 and in terms of dramatic events, famous personalities or note-worthy buildings his criticism had some justification. Nevertheless Dorking has survived for nearly two millennia, and modern research is beginning to reveal much of the story of this small town. Our perception of the early centuries is understandably dim, but from the later Middle Ages Dorking men and women can be discerned going about their daily business, plying their trades, practising their religion, brawling, gambling, marrying and dying, and always in the background is the market which was for so long the chief reason for the town's existence. Few of these people became household names but together they played an essential part in the nation's history.

Antiquities may still not be too obvious but they can be seen, and recent archaeological excavations have uncovered the remains of Roman settlement and part of the medieval graveyard. Even modern buildings are not always what they seem; the Victorians demolished the medieval church, but they only refronted many of the shops and houses in the High Street, and there are surprises to be found behind their facades.

A fully comprehensive history covering the whole manor and parish of Dorking, incorporating all the information now available, must be a long-term project. In the meantime, it is hoped that this concise account, which is limited to Dorking town, will help those who wish to learn more of its past. In a work of this scale it is not possible to give full references, but a list of sources and suggestions for further reading will be found at the back.

Buildings are identified by their current street numbers, which are likely to be more permanent than many of the establishments now, occupying the premises, although occasionally in the past the local council has introduced a programme of re-numbering and could do so again. The streets too are referred to by their modern names, though some of these would not have been recognised two hundred years ago. The High Street used to be East Street, Church Street was the Back Lane, North Street was merely a nameless thoroughfare, and Dene Street was originally Chergate or Chertgate Lane before becoming Ram Alley in the 17th century. Other changes have been Pip Lane to London Road, Downs Lane to Station Road, Strood Lane to Pixham Lane and Sandy (or Sandy Cross) Lane to Vincent's and Coldharbour Lanes.

For the sake of comparison, an attempt has been made throughout to estimate population figures, but not too much reliance should be placed on the earlier ones as they are based on information which may not show the whole picture.

We are grateful to his Grace the Duke of Norfolk, the Surrey Record Office, the Surrey Archaeological Society and the Dorking & District Museum for allowing access to their archives and collections, and to the latter, John Coombes, David Knight, Pip Mee and N E C (Ted) Molyneux for making illustrations available. Thanks are due to Beryl Higgins for so patiently translating our rough sketches into neat maps. Mary Day worked valiantly to search out and arrange illustrations. Michael Elphick contributed valuable advice on mills and the workhouses and James Berry-Clarke helped with photographic work. We have made good use of Allan Brigham's original research on 19th century housing development, and David Timperley, Head of Housing Services, Mole Valley District Council supplied details of council housing. Finally, Ethel Clear, Edith and Doris Mercer and Lionel Green gave up time to read our drafts, making helpful suggestions. We also acknowledge with appreciation an ex gratia payment of £200 by Mole Valley District Council towards our production costs.

VIVIEN ETTLINGER
BRIAN OVERELL
ALAN A JACKSON

Dorking,
July 1991

CHAPTER ONE

THE EARLY SETTLEMENT AND MANOR

Vivien Ettlinger

The site

Dorking lies on the lower greensand between the chalk slopes of the North Downs and the clay of the Low Weald. The low sandy hills of the Nower, Glory Wood and Deepdene frame the town to the south, while a few miles to the south-west Leith Hill rises to a height of nearly 300 metres. North of the High Street the Pippbrook flows through its associated alluviums and gravels and a narrow band of gault clay to join the river Mole near Pixham. The town stands at a point where a convenient route running along the foot of the chalk escarpment, today used by the A25 and the Redhill to Guildford railway, passes across the gap cut by the Mole through the North Downs which now accommodates the A24 and the Leatherhead to Horsham railway.

Early visitors

Evidence for the presence, even if transitory, of prehistoric man in the neighbourhood, is provided by the numbers of mesolithic and neolithic flints which can be found on the sandy soils to the south of the town. Bronze Age people stayed long enough to construct round barrows on Milton Heath and The Glory, neither so far excavated. The Iron Age stronghold of Anstiebury dates from the 1st century BC but it is not known where its builders, the native British inhabitants, lived and farmed.

A Roman Settlement

The earliest evidence for settlement in Dorking town is Roman. The great military road constructed in the 1st century AD to carry supplies from Chichester to London, later called Stane Street by the Saxons, passed through the centre of the town. It has been identified in several places; at North Holmwood and in Horsham Road as it approached South Street, and again where it crossed the north-west corner of the churchyard making for the Mole crossing at Burford, though the precise route through the town is not known. It seems likely that the Romans would have established a posting station at such a suitable place and recent excavations in the Church Street area and to the north-east of the church have proved the existence of Romano-British occupation of some kind from the 1st to the 4th centuries AD. So far the remains consist of pits and ditches but the presence in them of building tiles, luxury pottery and jewellery suggests at least one substantial building.

Although the importance of Stane Street as a long distance route declined quite early in the Roman period, it no doubt continued to be used locally by the natives. As Dorking also lay directly between villas at Abinger and Walton Hill and a possible settlement at Betchworth, it is conceivable that its later role was that of a market. Whatever the truth Dorking, with the rest of England, sank into obscurity during the Dark Ages which followed the withdrawal of the Roman legions, and unsubstantiated tales of Danish pillagers notwithstanding, did not emerge into recorded history for another six hundred years.

The first Dorkinians?

There is one slight thread of continuity and that lies in the name itself. Dorking probably means 'the people of Deorc' and the second syllable derives from the Saxon place-name element 'ingas' implying an origin in the 7th or 8th centuries. However, Deorc is not Saxon, and it is just possible that it refers to the native Britons still living in the settlement when the Saxons arrived.

Domesday Dorking

The King holds Dorking in demesne

The first historical reference to the manor is in the Domesday Survey of 1086 where it appears as *Dorchinges,* and probably embraced the modern parishes of Dorking, Capel and the Holmwoods. It was then in the hands of the king, William the Conqueror, who had assumed the lordship in 1075 on the death of Edith, widow of Edward the Confessor. There is reason to believe that both manor and parish had previously been part of an extensive Saxon royal estate centred on Leatherhead.

Details in the Domesday entry are brief and any description of Dorking at this early date can only be speculative. There was a church, probably on or near the present site, and it is reasonable to assume that the village lay around this, close to the highway between Reigate and Guildford. Near the church would have been the manor farm and buildings with accommodation for the four families of serfs who tended the lord's land and livestock, and not far away the homes and small plots of the 13 families of bordars or cottagers who worked for hire and were allowed to graze their swine on the Cotmandene. There were three watermills on the Pippbrook, and north of the stream on the fertile loam lay the lordship lands and common fields.

The majority of the tenants were villeins, 38 families who supported themselves off the 60 or so acres each held in return for rendering services to their lord. Their homesteads and lands lay along the tracks leading south from the settlement, on the slopes of Leith Hill, and in clearings in the Wealden forest which still covered much of modern Capel. Huge areas of heath and woodland would have surrounded the cultivated lands, with the largely untouched Homewood (as Holmwood was spelt until the end of the 16th century) almost dividing the manor in two. On these so-called commons or wastes, the tenants could graze their animals, and enjoy other customary rights such as collecting wood for house building and fuel.

Attached to the main manor there were two small independent estates held respectively by Richard of Clare and Odo, Bishop of Bayeux. Neither has been positively identified, but it is likely that the former was the 'sub-manor' of Hamsted, which lay to the south-west of the settlement and whose name is perpetuated in the present Hampstead Lane; the other may have been Bradley on the northern border which is similarly commemorated. Both were absorbed later into the Manor of Dorking.

Seal of John de Warenne, Earl of Surrey and Sussex (1286–1347).

In about 1089 the manor was granted by William Rufus to William de Warenne, a Norman baron with royal connections, and it has remained almost continuously in the lordship of the Warennes and their descendants until the present day, when the Lord of the Manor is the Duke of Norfolk. The Warennes were Lords of Lewes and Earls of Surrey as well as holding vast estates in other parts of the country. Their Surrey seat was Reigate Castle from where their officers could keep a watchful, even predatory, eye on Dorking. In 1235 their bailiffs were accused of seizing corn there against the will of those to whom it belonged, and as late as 1385 the unfortunate John atte Chert of Dorking was imprisoned in Reigate Castle until he paid a fine of one hundred shillings for hunting on his own freehold property.

Military matters

The Earls generally supported the Norman and Plantagenet kings in their many disputes at home and abroad, and although the manor's principal value was as a source of income and household supply, tenants may also have been called on to serve under the Warenne standard of blue and gold chequers in places as far away as France, Scotland or Wales.

Little is known of events in Dorking until the end of the 13th century. Most manorial records have not survived, if they ever existed, and references at a national level are few. In 1216 a few months before King John died, the Dauphin of France, who had been invited over by the rebel barons, must have created some local excitement when he passed through Dorking on his way to Guildford after investing Reigate Castle. The following year, the nine year old Henry III with the regent, William Marshall, Earl of Pembroke, followed the same route but paused in the manor long enough to issue a rallying call to his supporters before continuing on his successful campaign to oust the French army.

Homicide and a hermit

Other events were less dramatic, consisting chiefly of land deals and dreary wrangles over property, though there were some criminal cases. In 1241 a chaplain by the name of Vivian was discovered with his neck broken in the house of a Dorking man called Payan Wrang, who was found guilty of the murder. This house can probably be identified with the earliest recorded secular building in the town, which stood at the back of the present White Horse Hotel. It had been granted freely, together with Payan himself, by Earl Warenne to the Knights Templar and after they were suppressed in 1308 it had passed to the Knights of St John and was known as the Cross House after the emblem of their Order. Oddly enough, the house was the scene of more violence in 1520 when it was occupied by the vicar, Miles Hogg, and an armed gang broke in to attack his servant. Not until the 18th century was the frontage developed and it became a hostelry.

There is also a mystery. In 1240 a grant was made to the 'recluse of Dorking' of a yearly allowance of wood for a fire. Was there a local hermit or anchorite and if so, where did they live? In the later Middle Ages there are several references to a close called Ankershagh lying near the manor buildings but nothing more is known.

CHAPTER TWO

MEDIEVAL MANOR AND MARKET: 1300–1485

Vivien Ettlinger

Market rights

In 1278 the manor was held by Earl John de Warenne, who was later to distinguish himself in Edward I's wars against the Welsh and Scots. In response to a royal enquiry, he defiantly claimed his lands by right of the sword with which his ancestor had supported William the Conqueror, and his claim was confirmed by charter. As well as lordship of the land and tenants, his immemorial rights in Dorking, which in legal terms meant since 1189, included the holding of a twice-weekly market on Mondays and Thursdays, and an annual fair on the Eve and Day of Ascension. This is the clue to Dorking's later status as one of the comparatively few towns in Surrey. Although not politically or industrially important, it was a market centre for the surrounding villages and hamlets, and perhaps an even wider area. As early as 1277, officials from the manor of Farleigh near Croydon were buying iron and horseshoes at Dorking.

Many manorial records survive from the early 14th century onwards, and it is clear that by this time Dorking, in common with the rest of the south-east, had a greatly increased population and considerably more land under cultivation than at Domesday. The isolated farms in the south of the manor, many of them bearing familiar names such as Holloway, Goodwins, Stubbs, Breakespeares, Aldhurst, and Beare, had spread to meet each other. Acres of the heath and woodland had been ploughed up, and the standing timber was being steadily depleted.

The manor was divided into four tithings or burghs for local administrative purposes. Chippingburgh comprised West Street, Butter Hill and South Street, Eastburgh ran from Pump Corner to London Road, and Foreignburgh, later called Holmwood, embraced all the outlying areas as far south as Betchets Green (South Holmwood). The fourth, Waldburgh, was later called Capel in recognition of the parish created there around the church, originally a chapel attached to Dorking church. (When the manors of Milton and Westcott were absorbed into Dorking in the 17th century, they too became burghs.)

The two smaller but more densely populated burghs, Chipping (a Saxon word meaning market) and East, together formed the nucleus of the future town, which was described in contemporary documents as a vill, implying a somewhat lesser status. Unlike many places of comparable size in the country, Dorking was never granted a borough charter and remained in the control of the lord of the manor throughout the Middle

Ages, relying on his right to hold a market and fair for its economic prosperity.

The open market place stretched from Butter Hill to West Street, surrounding the well at Pump Corner, and by 1400 there were references to shops in the 'new market', suggesting that business had started to expand east. On both sides of the main highways which now formed the familiar Y-shape, smiths, skinners, weavers, tailors, shoemakers and other leatherworkers lived and worked. Down by the Pippbrook, two of the lord's mills ground the tenants' corn in return for a percentage of the flour, tanners processed hides, and fullers and dyers finished cloth, while nearer the centre, bakers, brewers and butchers catered for the inhabitants as well as visitors to market and fair. Fish was caught in the short length of the Mole described in 1430 as being from 'a certain place called le Swolowe to Markereslane' which had been allocated by the lord for the use of his tenants.

Inns

Dorking lay on the main route between the shrines of St. Swithin at Winchester and St. Thomas à Becket at Canterbury, and for travellers on pilgrimage or merchants on business there were two inns, the Cardinal's Hat and the George. Painted beams and other vestiges of the latter are still carefully protected in the front upper room of 47 High Street. On the other side of the street at what is now Nos 108–116, the Cardinal's Hat, after a period as a private residence, was rebuilt in the late 17th century to become the Red Lion.

Customary duties

There were no longer any serfs but the majority of tenants were still bound by custom to the manor, which they might not leave without licence. Permission was also needed to marry, and on the death of a tenant, the lord claimed a heriot, namely, his best beast. (The second best was the perquisite of the vicar). The number of farms held by villein families had changed little from the 38 recorded at Domesday and although most rents and services had now been commuted into money, these tenants still had some duties to perform. Timber and charcoal from the Homewood and Ashcombe Wood had to be carried on wagons to Kingston or Thames Ditton for the passage by barge to the lord's household in London, and wool from his sheep taken to his store at Reigate Castle. In addition, each year these men had to elect from amongst their number a reeve to be answerable to the lord for rent collection, the management of the manor farm and general day to day administration of the manor.

The cottagers, still 13 as recorded at Domesday, supplied seasonal help on the manor farm, and their Christmas dinner at three halfpence a head was an annual item in the expense accounts. They had also to take their turn at beadle service, which involved assisting the reeve, enforcing orders made at the manor court, and guarding prisoners and taking them to Guildford gaol or Reigate Castle depending on the nature of the crime.

Two substantial estates, Bonnets in Capel and Chert* in Dorking were each held freely for an annual rent of a pair of spurs price sixpence, which suggests that they had originally been granted in return for military service. Much property too was now held by freeholders, many of them wealthy non-residents, professional men or merchants looking for an investment, who installed sub-tenants on their land or in their shops in the township.

People were also leaving Dorking. By the custom of the manor, property that was not freehold was inherited by the youngest son, a Saxon practice known as Borough English, which left elder sons to fend for themselves. Some acquired freehold property, but others anticipated Dick Whittington and headed for London to make their fortunes. Some time in the 13th century, two manor tenants called John and Odo atte Dene de Dorkyng apparently took this course and established themselves as wool merchants in the city so successfully that in 1343 there was a Dorkynggeslane in the City parish of St. Martin Vintry where they lived.

The Manor Court

All male tenants over the age of 12 were obliged to attend the court presided over by the lord's steward when he visited the manor every three weeks. He would have used the small manor house consisting of a hall with an upper room which lay near the lord's oxshed and other farm buildings in the manor grounds. These were between the church and Mill Lane, and the people probably assembled in the open space still called Court Close in the 18th century, to be summoned before the official when their cases came up. Here they would seek approval for land transfers, apply and pay for licences to marry or live outside the manor, and answer for breaches of the law or manorial custom and other misdemeanours. Unless required to present themselves in person to answer for some wrong-doing, women did not attend these courts but were represented by a male relative or friend.

Common offences were brewing ale without licence, selling underweight bread or putrid food, trespass, scraps between neighbours, felling timber without permission and poaching. Rabbits had been introduced to the manor perhaps as early as the 12th century, but these desirable

* The name Chert, meaning a rough common, was so spelt until the early modern period. It was transferred to an adjoining property Chart Park, in the 18th century and is recalled in the modern Chart Downs and Chart Lane.

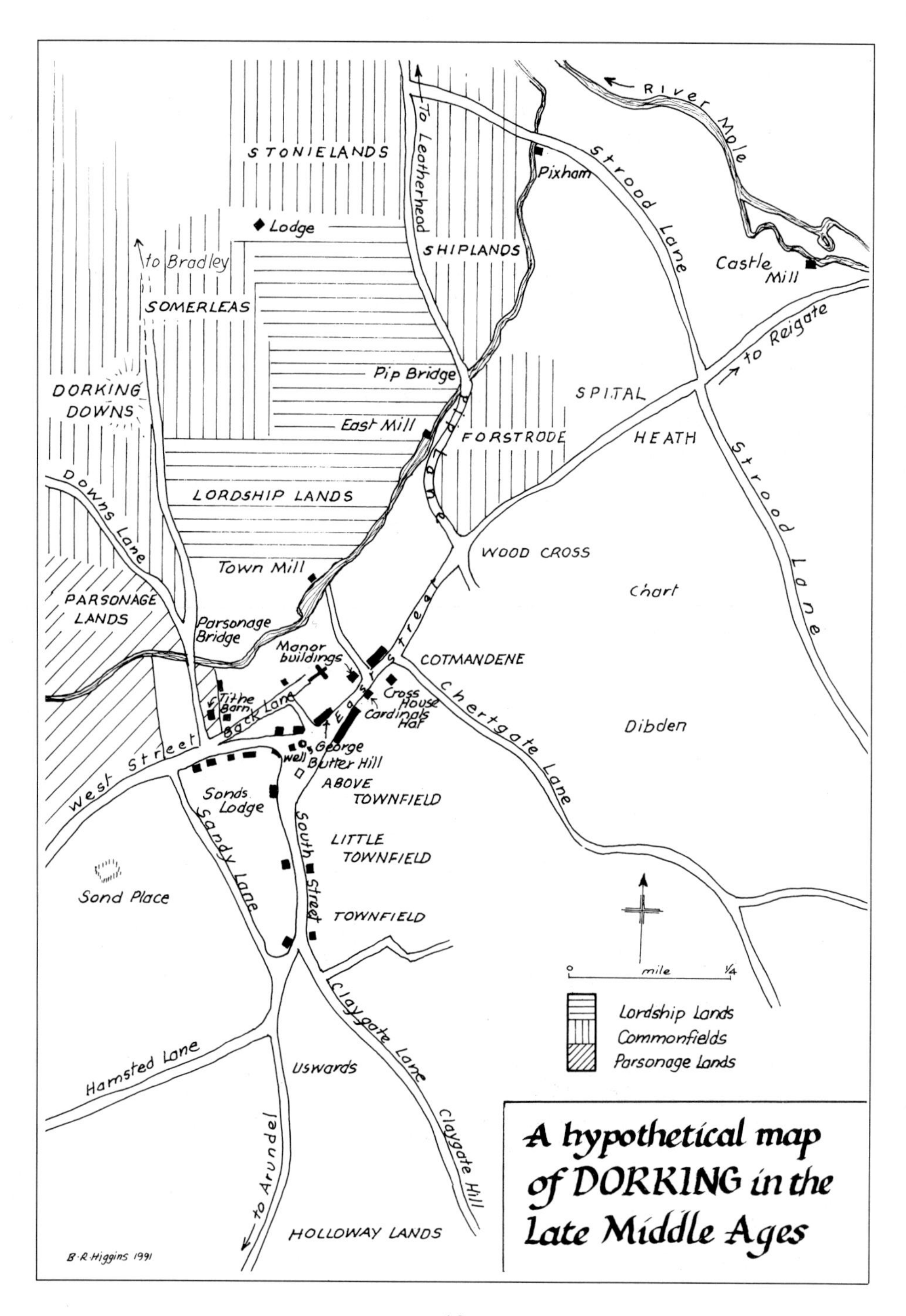

A hypothetical map of DORKING in the Late Middle Ages

additions to the larder were guarded jealously by the lord's warrener from his lodge on the hill at the end of what is now Keppel Road. Tenants who ventured out with dogs, ferrets and nets were fined heavily. There were also repeated prosecutions for blocking the gutters and dumping obnoxious refuse from houses, shops and shambles into the streets, typical medieval practices which contributed little to the health and convenience of the inhabitants.

Fines were imposed for the majority of offences, but there were some crimes that merited sterner retribution. In 1373 John Smith was convicted of being a petty pyker or thief and sentenced to the pillory. For night prowling and waking up the neighbours by firing his crossbow, Thomas A Stone too suffered the pillory and was fined as well. At the same court Margaret Brugges was condemned to the ducking-stool, the usual penalty for being a common scold, though even this could be avoided by paying a large enough fine. The lord may have been keen to maintain law and order, but he was equally interested in making a profit.

The second church

The architecture of the now-demolished medieval church suggested that it originated in the 12th century, replacing the building mentioned

Medieval Church from the south-west shortly before demolition. *Drawing by unknown artist. (Photograph Pip Mee).*

at Domesday. In about 1140 Countess Isabel de Warenne, widow of the second earl, had granted the church of Dorking to the Priory of St. Pancras at Lewes, an earlier Warenne foundation, and it is probable that either she or the new patrons were responsible for the reconstruction. With the grant went the tithes and the rectory or parsonage lands which lay in a block between the Westcott Road and the Pippbrook, as well as the tithe barn and yard standing at the north-east corner of what are now Station Road and Church Street.

The Priory also acquired the right to present the priest, and may have been responsible for the appointment of William, the first recorded holder of the office, but little is known of the early clergy, and that little is hardly to their credit. In 1284 the rectory was held by Bogo de Clare, son of the Earl of Gloucester and a prebendary of York. An unscrupulous cleric, he was notorious for collecting offices and rectories as well as any other property he could lay his hands on. It is unlikely that he ever came near the place, merely enjoying the tithes, as his household accounts mention mutton, pork and corn from his store at Dorking. Bogo died in 1294, only to be replaced as rector by John de Warenne, probably an illegitimate son of the earl, who was not even an ordained priest, and certainly not resident. He too regarded the parish rents and tithes strictly as personal income. He was continually in debt and on several occasions the local populace was treated to the unedifying, though no doubt entertaining, spectacle of the rector's servants and the sheriff's posse battling over the hay and corn stored in the tithe barn.

In 1334 the church was conveyed to the Priory of the Holy Cross, Reigate, in whose hands the spiritual well-being of Dorking was better regulated. The Prior assumed the rectorship himself but appointed a regular succession of well-educated vicars. Most of them were resident though not always in the same house, and it seems that there was no official vicarage at this time. The pastoral qualities of these clerics are unrecorded but they were certainly active in the community, buying and selling property and even becoming involved in brawls.

Fraternity of the Blessed Mary

A number of improvements and alterations to the church building now followed, the most radical occurring in the late 14th century when a clerestory and two side aisles were added to the nave. In the north aisle was an altar with a painting of the Virgin Mary and this may have been connected with a guild or brotherhood dedicated to the Blessed Mary. Dorking was too small a community to support craft guilds such as were found in London and large towns, but followed the example of many parishes at this time and founded a religious guild or brotherhood. This was supported by some at least of the wealthier parishioners and its principal object was 'towardes the findinge of one prieste to praye for the soules of the brotheren and systers of the same fraternitie for ever', but it may also be thought of as a mutual benefit society. To this end, as well as an annual subscription to meet the priest's stipend, members donated or bequeathed money and property, and sometimes indulged in fund-raising events called church ales. There are several early 16th century references to a cottage called a yeld (or gild) house on the site of what is now No. 21 High Street, and this could have been the scene of such jollifications.

The Sondes family and the decline of the manor

Major national disasters like civil war, harvest failures and plague epidemics, even the Black Death of 1348, pass unremarked in the local records, but their consequences may be detected in the economy. By the end of the 14th century labour shortage was responsible for a huge increase in sheep farming on the lordship lands at the expense of arable, and smaller farmers followed suit. Much land and property lay unoccupied and when a tenant was persuaded to take it, it was generally at a reduced rent. Those tenants who survived therefore were able to enlarge their holdings on very favourable terms, and foremost among them were the Sondes, who had been acquiring land in the manor for centuries, and whose name is perpetuated in Sondes Place Farm.

By the mid–15th century the lordship had become divided between several female descendants of the Warennes who had no direct interest in the manor beyond receiving their share of the revenues. Sheep had proved an uncertain investment due to the prevalence of disease and the lordship lands had been let to the Sondes, who had also purchased the Bradley estate, mentioned in Chapter 1. The Sondes were now a family of some consequence, and apparently led the local support for Jack Cade's Kentish rebellion in the summer of 1450. Amongst the pardons issued afterwards were ones for Henry Sonde, gentleman, and two yeomen, two farmers and five leading tradesmen, all of Dorking, for 'gathering together against the statutes of the realm to the contempt of the king's estate'. This may have been the same Henry Sonde who died in 1464 leaving money to the church, a great log to make a ladder to the belfry, and an ox for the use of the Fraternity of the Blessed Mary. In his will he refers to the church simply as the church of Dorking, as was the usual custom, and not until 1486, again in a will, is the dedication to St. Martin first mentioned.

The mood of the times coupled with the greater economic independence of so many of their tenants ensured that by the end of the Middle Ages the lords' powers over life and limb had almost vanished. In Dorking, manor courts were held less frequently and the manor buildings were dismantled, the Horsham stone from the roofs being disposed of eventually for use on Betchworth Castle, Mickleham Hall and other buildings in the vicinity.

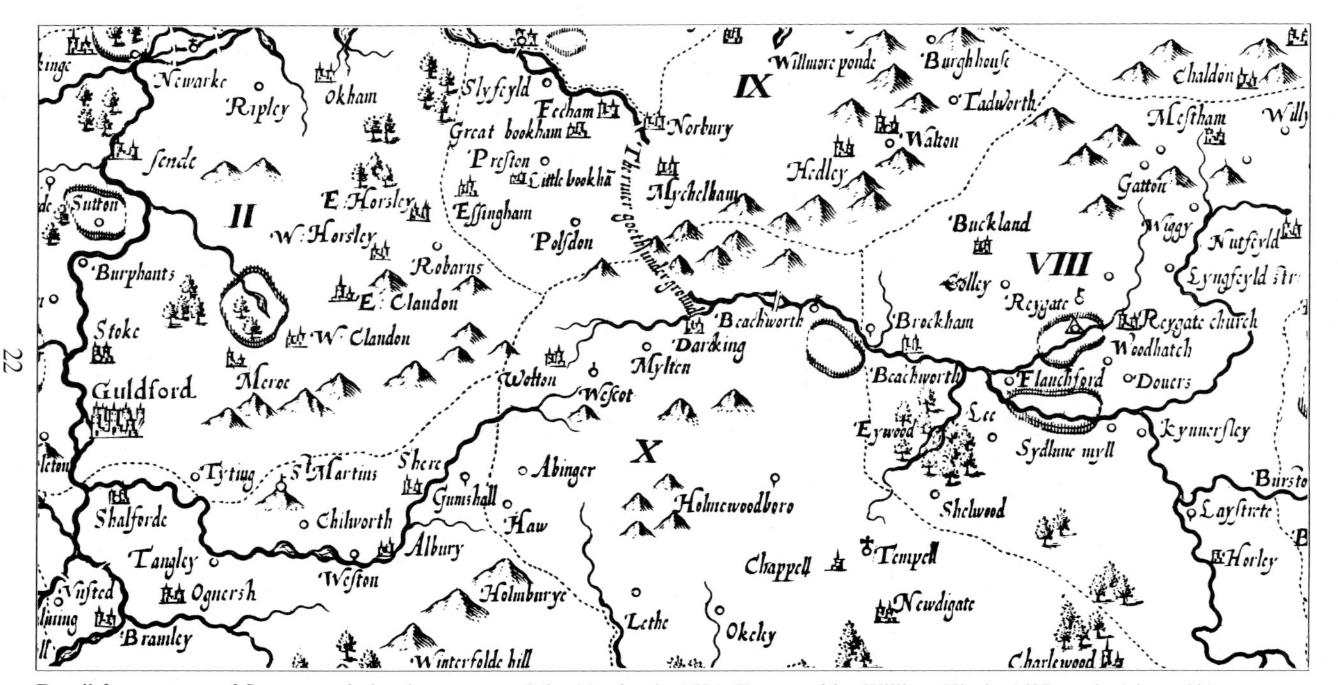

Detail from a map of Surrey made by the surveyor John Norden in 1594. Engraved by William Kip in 1607, scale 1 in = 2½m approx.

CHAPTER THREE

TUDOR AND EARLY STUART TOWN: 1486–1642

Vivien Ettlinger

Arrival of the gentry

Peace and strong government under the Tudors brought prosperity to the nation; the town, as it soon might properly be called, started to grow. After a successful marriage alliance with a Kentish family, the Sondes left Dorking, and although they retained property in the district for many years, they had little local influence. The gap was filled by the Brownes of Betchworth Castle who, as stewards to the absentee lords, gradually acquired property in the manor, and in 1586 purchased a fourth part of the lordship. Their relatives and friends moved into the town and were joined by other courtiers, merchants and businessmen who had benefited from the national rise in fortune, and were anxious to live away from the now overcrowded cities of London and Westminster. William Henn, who had been a purveyor of butter to the king, appropriately enough built a house on Butter Hill (the name was in fact used much earlier and could be a corruption of Burgh Hill) and William Sackville, a former train-bearer to Queen Mary, became another resident. Local tradesmen like the Goodwyns were also bettering themselves through commercial astuteness and judicious marriages. So the process of gentrification began.

Business booms

From an estimated total of 800–900 inhabitants in the parish when registers were introduced in 1538, the population climbed steadily to nearly 1,400 by the end of the century, in spite of set-backs caused by epidemics. Demand for luxury goods led to an increase in trades like weaving, tailoring and shoe-making and new ones such as glove-making were introduced. Drapers set up shop to retail the finer fabrics that were now available, and grocers purveyed spices imported from the New World. The market had long since overflowed its old venue around Pump Corner, and in the 1590s a market house was erected further east along the High Street to cope with the abundant grain coming in from the surrounding farms.

As the century progressed, less and less of this grain was being ground in the two lordship mills, one on the north bank of the stream opposite Mill Lane, and the other at the bend in London Road, and by the 1570s both had ceased to function and the millstones sold. Court fines for using alternative mills, thus depriving the lord of his toll, had become increasingly common, and Milton mill is mentioned on occasion. There was still the Sondes' mill at Pixham, and the Brownes owned Castle mill but some of the competition may have come from a windmill

Market House. *Water colour by John Hassell. (Surrey Archaeological Society).*

on Tower Hill which must have been in use at about this time. The mill in London Road was rebuilt and flourished again in the early 18th century, but the town mill disappeared for ever and today its millpond is Meadowbank football ground.

Houses and shops proliferated; existing buildings along the main streets were sub-divided and vacant plots developed. Building skills were in demand, and timber from the Holmwood not only supplied the framework for many new houses locally, but was also carried the 12 miles to Ewell, where Henry VIII was constructing his magnificent palace of Nonsuch.

War and rumours of war

Throughout the 16th century the threat of war was never far away, first against the French and then the Spanish, and the government kept lists of able-bodied men who were to be mustered in a national emergency. Each had to provide himself with a bow and arrows and practise regularly at the archery butts off Dene Street, or Ram Alley as it was then known. To ensure compliance, other sports and pastimes were forbidden though the ban was not wholly successful. Many Dorking men were fined at the manor court for playing bowls or dicing, and in 1531 William Wheler, a tailor and draper, was found guilty of 'Tenys pley' with nine companions in the market place. In 1588, when the Armada was finally sighted in the Channel, 800 men from the neighbourhood were ordered to muster at Dorking from where they marched to Chatham, though their services were not called upon, and as soon as the danger had passed, they were dismissed summarily to make their own way home.

A Protestant priest

Apparently the establishment of the Church of England caused little problem in Dorking. The forced transfer of the parsonage lands from Reigate Priory to Lord William Howard probably left the parishioners unmoved, although the confiscation of church plate and the suppression of the Brotherhood and forfeiture of its property must have been resented. A church stripped of so much of its accustomed colour and light may have seemed strange, and the reforms and counter-reforms of Henry VIII, Edward VI and Mary bewildering, but by the more tolerant reign of Elizabeth I the parish had settled down under Stephen Richman, a married vicar with pronounced Protestant views. In 1578 he was indicted at the Assizes for refusing to wear a surplice, and again four years later for clerical non-conformity.

Vestry government

Lay authority was also changing. The Tudors favoured central government and with the decay of the manorial system they turned to the parish to implement their ordinances. Churchwardens had existed in Dorking since the Middle Ages, when they had been elected to look after the church building and goods. The earliest recorded holders of the office were John Carpenter and Robert Ashcombe who in 1400 had attempted to recover money borrowed from the parish chest. Now the churchwardens and parishioners, together forming a body called the Vestry after the room in which they usually met, became the local authority for the town and parish and gradually assumed most of the functions of the manor court excepting those connected with the lord's rents and property. In the three centuries before a district council was established, the Vestry became responsible for highways, health, services and many other matters, one of the most burdensome being the care of the poor and needy.

Poor relief

In spite of the prosperity of many under the Tudor monarchs, the country experienced over-crowding, disease, war and ever-rising inflation, and in Dorking as elsewhere the proportion of poor, sick and disabled rose alarmingly. Money and property donated to the church for charitable purposes had been confiscated at the Reformation. The Brotherhood lands and tenements had been sold by the Crown Commissioners to the Brownes, and one property which was described as 'the house in which a poor man dwells' may have been an almshouse. Elizabeth's government feared popular unrest and legislated to remedy the situation. The task of setting a poor rate, collecting it from the better-off parishioners, and applying it to the relief of the needy fell on St. Martin's Vestry.

In fairness, it should also be said that Richard Browne returned part of the Brotherhood property to the parish in 1613 to be used as Dorking's first known almshouses. These were eight tenements built on the site of 122–130 South Street, and became the first workhouse when new almshouses were built on Cotmandene at the beginning of the 18th century.

A Pilgrim Father

One of the more impressive town houses built at the beginning of the 17th century was occupied by William Mullins, a shoemaker, who in 1620 sailed on the *Mayflower* with his wife and two youngest children.

Shortly after their arrival in New Plymouth, most of the family succumbed to illness aggravated by the harsh conditions, and only a daughter, Priscilla, survived. She later married another emigrant called John Alden and his wooing is immortalised, though probably apocryphally, in *The Courtship of Miles Standish,* a poem by Longfellow.

Archly the maiden smiled, and with eyes over-running with laughter,

Said, in a tremulous voice, 'Why don't you speak for yourself, John?'

Mullins' four-gabled house still stands, now shared by four antique shops, at Nos. 58–61 West Street. It is said to be the only known surviving home in this country of a Pilgrim Father.

More Inns

The medieval inns had not survived into the Tudor period though, as the numerous fines imposed at the manor court bear witness, brewing both for domestic consumption and for sale in alehouses continued unabated. The addition of hops to ale to produce the more fashionable beer demanded a more complicated manufacturing process than a supply of water and a wash-tub in the back yard, and malthouses and brewhouses were added to many of the premises in the town.

By the end of the 16th century larger establishments were needed to cater for increasing travel on business and pleasure, sometimes now by private coach, and in the 1590s Edward Goodwyn opened the Queen's Arms, later to be called the King's Arms in honour of a new monarch. An extensive building stretching from the corner of North Street as far as Mullins' house in West Street, with stables, yards, outbuildings and a bowling alley, this probably continued as an inn until the early 18th century. Goodwyn's initials can still be seen carved on a window bracket at the back. It was soon followed by the Chequers on the site of Nos. 20–28 High Street, and the Lower Chequers, later to be known as the

King's Head, on the corner of High Street and North Street, where much of the original building is still visible. The Chequers had ceased to be an inn by the mid 18th century and was demolished in 1968, but areas of painted wall plaster were preserved and can be seen in the shop now standing on the site.

Smith's Charity

In spite of these signs of affluence, the poor continued to be a drain on the parishioners' pockets. The poor rate quadrupled in the first 70 years of the 17th century and Dorking was fortunate to become a major beneficiary of the Surrey philanthropist, Henry Smith of Wandsworth. He was a silversmith and Alderman of the City of London who, before his death in 1627, gave £1,000 each to Dorking and four other towns in the county. This was to be invested in land to provide an income for the relief of the poor and for setting them to work. Dorking Vestry invested the gift in some property at Bottesford, Leicestershire and although it has since been sold, the proceeds are still used for the benefit of the almshouses.

House of the Puritan William Mullins in West Street. *Postcard dated c. 1938*

CHAPTER FOUR

COMMONWEALTH AND RESTORATION DORKING: 1643-1688

Vivien Ettlinger

Civil War

It seems unlikely to have been religious persecution that drove a wealthy tradesman like William Mullins to the New World. There were many like him in Dorking and the evidence points to the town's having Puritan sympathies. The number of new gentry had also risen, but these were mostly self-made men whose concern was more with the effect on their purses of rising prices and heavy taxes than with the divine right of kings. When civil war broke out in 1642 Dorking followed the rest of Surrey in supporting Parliament, and those who had reservations kept a diplomatic silence. Amongst these was Sir Ambrose Browne of Betchworth Castle who managed to smuggle a troop of horses to the king at Oxford whilst at the same time acting as a Parliamentary Commissioner for the county.

Local enthusiasm for the war was never more than luke-warm and by 1648 the townspeople were weary of paying still higher taxes, including swingeing excise duty on tobacco, liquor and many comestibles. They resented the conscription of their horses, and all the ills attendant upon having Cromwell's soldiers billetted on them. This last was a particular grievance because it strained the accommodation and food resources. It also increased the risk of infection from plague (1643 and 1647 were very bad years for this in Dorking, as elsewhere in Surrey), and it introduced a violent element into the community. The burial register records one soldier whose brains were blown out by a musket, and another who was slain by a comrade. The knights and gentlemen of Surrey met at Dorking on 8 May 1648 to prepare a petition demanding that King and Parliament be reconciled and their armies disbanded and paid off. Some days later the petitioners assembled on Putney Heath and marched to Westminster to present their demand but on the way they were joined by some rabble, the demonstration got out of hand, and most were lucky to escape with their lives.

Although Dorking must have been used to seeing detachments of soldiers in the streets, the closest the town came to the fighting was also in 1648 when an ill-judged Royalist rising led by the Earl of Holland set up headquarters briefly at Reigate. On 6 July part of this force marched to Dorking hoping to raise some support but, as the official report says, 'found some arms yet little care was taken to arm the foot that came with us, or to mount some gentlemen that waited for that purpose'.

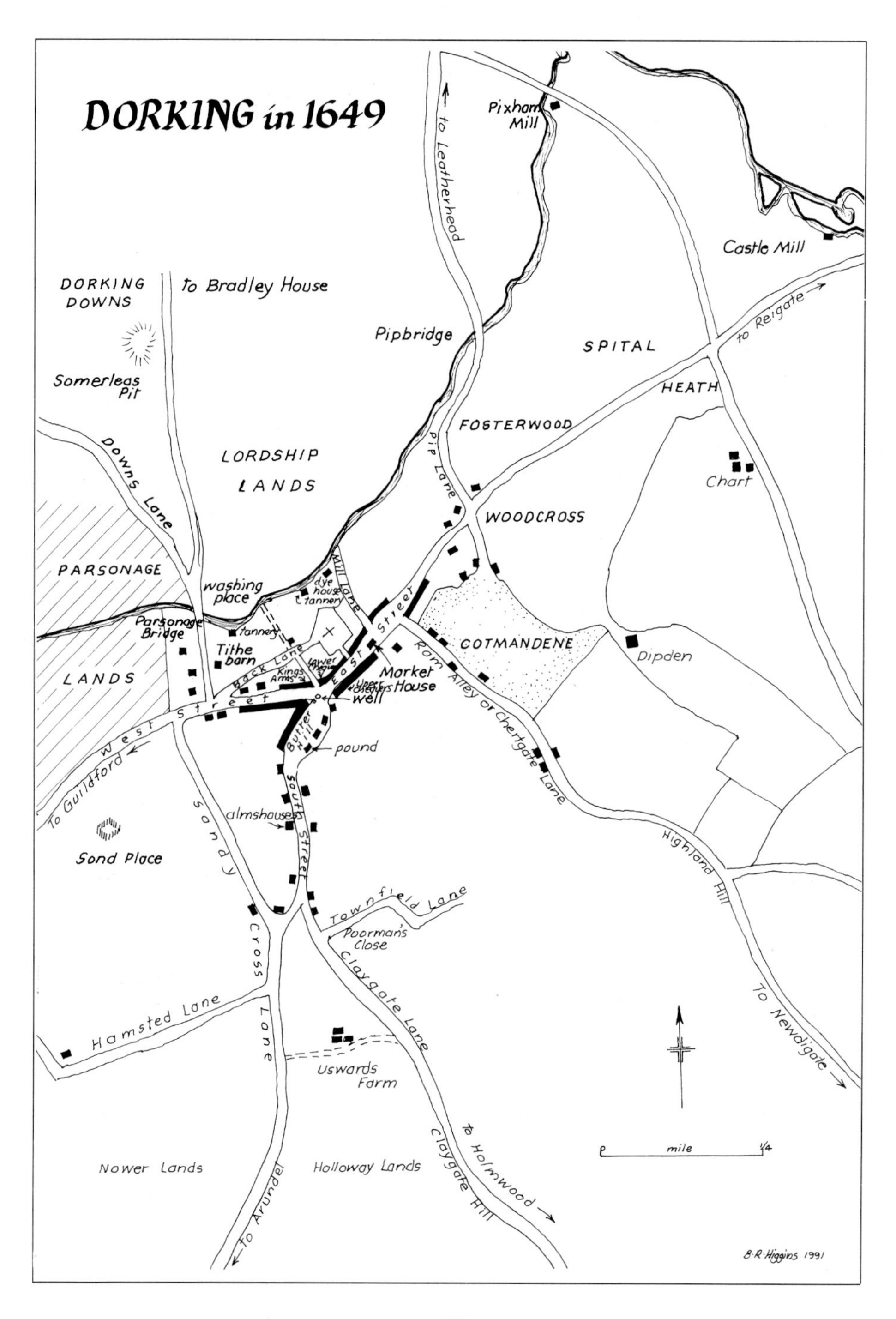
DORKING in 1649
Pixham Mill
to Leatherhead
Castle Mill
DORKING DOWNS
to Bradley House
to Reigate
Pipbridge
SPITAL
HEATH
Somerleas Pit
FOSTERWOOD
Downs Lane
LORDSHIP
LANDS
Pip Lane
Chart
WOODCROSS
PARSONAGE
washing place
dye house
tannery
Mill Lane
Parsonage Bridge
tannery
East Street
COTMANDENE
Tithe barn
Back Lane
Kings Arms
Market House
Dipden
LANDS
Upper Chequers
well
Ram Alley or Chertgate Lane
West Street
to Guildford
Butter Hill
pound
South Street
Sandy Cross Lane
almshouses
Sand Place
Highland Hill
Townfield Lane
Poorman's Close
Claygate Lane
To Newdigate
Hamsted Lane
Uswards Farm
mile 1/4
to Holmwood
Nower Lands
Holloway Lands
Claygate Hill
to Arundel
B·R·Higgins 1991

Although Sir Ambrose Browne's son, Adam, was a colonel in Holland's army, this rebuff undoubtedly reflected the prevailing sentiments of the townspeople; many of them inclined towards Puritanism and most were heartily sick of the war. Holland's men retreated to Reigate, and were chased to Surbiton by Parliament troops, where they were decisively defeated.

A Survey of the Manor

During the first half of the 17th century the Howard family gradually acquired all three parts of the lordship not in the possession of the Brownes. In 1649, the year Charles I was executed, Henry Howard, Earl of Arundel and Surrey, presumably to establish the value of his new holding, commissioned from a William Forster a survey of the whole manor. This detailed every property with its name, location, area, annual rent, occupier, and sometimes past occupiers. Similar surveys had been made in the past and are the source of some of the earlier history, but this one was accompanied by the first known estate map, invaluable to Dorking historians as a basis for their research. A wry comment by William Forster in his introduction throws some light on the attitude of the locals: 'If the Condition of the Time and the perverse peevishness of some had not obstructed the same it had been fit and requisite that All as well Freeholders as Customary Tenants should have brought in their Evidence . . . and might have prevented many suits and much Trouble in Time to come . . . '

Dull days

Samuel Cosens, who had been instituted as vicar of St. Martin's in 1624, was a Puritan and retained his living under the Commonwealth, although both his church and his duties changed. Anything that smacked of popery had gone with the Reformation but now even the altar was replaced by a plain table, and services concentrated on the sermons delivered every Sunday from the hexagonal wooden pulpit which had been installed in 1637. Christmas was not celebrated, and marriages were strictly civil contracts made before a local Justice of the Peace, generally Lawrence Marsh, a merchant tailor from Highgate who had settled in Dorking in 1648. A staunch Puritan who served on a number of committees in Surrey under Cromwell, Marsh was one of the two county members in the Barebones Parliament in 1653. He lived in a house at the east end of the High Street (now Nos. 290–294) which was later enlarged and called Shrub Hill, and he continued to play a prominent part in local affairs until his death in 1665. In his will he left a ring to his 'Cousen Foe', probably James Foe, the father of Daniel Defoe, and James was later appointed executor to the will of Marsh's widow Elizabeth.

Defoe's Dorking

The inhabitants of Dorking must have welcomed the relaxation from austerity which followed the restoration of Charles II in 1660. Samuel Cosens died in 1661, leaving to the parish in which he had laboured so long 23 acres of land at Chislet in Kent. This is still administered for the benefit of the almshouses, and was the first of many subsequent local bequests. Cosens' demise made it easy to appoint a successor acceptable to the new government but other Puritan ministers were not so obliging; James Fisher, after his ejection from the living of Fetcham, came to Dorking and set up a school to which it is thought likely that Daniel Defoe was sent for a few years in the early 1670s. The connection between the Foe (the De- was added by Daniel) and Marsh families has been shown, and when writing about the town in his *Tour Through the Whole Island of Great Britain*, published in 1724, Defoe betrayed a knowledge of the place much greater than might be expected from a casual visitor.

The combination of pleasure-seeking, shrewd business and puritanism prevailing in the district at the time is aptly illustrated by an anecdote recounted by Defoe. Parties of fashionable people would travel from Epsom Spa to Box Hill on Sundays to disport themselves amongst the box bushes, and the enterprising innkeeper of the King's Arms in Dorking obtained permission from Sir Adam Browne to set up a supper club in a cave at the foot of a large beech tree on the summit. Word of this spread and attracted many of the local gentry until it became a scandal in the eyes of the more straitlaced Dorking youth, who complained of revelling and indecent mirth on the Sabbath. One Saturday night, therefore, some of them blew up the cave with gunpowder. Peace and purity then returned to Box Hill until the era of the day excursion.

Dissenters and Catholics

James Fisher lived in Spring Gardens, in a property called Barn Place which was owned by a nonconformist family of the name of Rose. He was one of several notable dissenters in the district, another being John Wood of Westcott. A third, the violent Fifth Monarchist Christopher Feake was arrested in Dorking in 1663 at a house he was alleged to have taken in another man's name, and where he had lived in great secrecy. Fisher was of a more peaceable nature and was noted for his 'humanity and tenderness'. An Independent meeting, or conventicle, met in his home and in 1669 the congregation was said to total about one hundred, presumably not all at the same time. At first such assemblies were unlawful but they were soon tolerated and were the forerunners of the thriving Congregational community with its own licensed meeting place which was established before the end of the 17th century.

Since Elizabeth's reign, Dorking had displayed a tendency towards the more extreme forms of Protestantism, and it is no surprise that according to a religious census in 1676, the parish contained 200 nonconformists out of a total of 1,218 possible churchgoers, a proportion much above the rest of the county. The total also included 18 Roman Catholics, families like the Stourtons, the Vauxs and the Belsons who had chosen Dorking as a discreet haven during the Commonwealth. The most notable of these was the Hon. Charles Howard of Greystoke, fourth son of Henry Frederick, Earl of Arundel, Surrey and Norfolk. Howard had inherited the small property known as the Deepdene in 1652, and proceeded to enlarge or rebuild the existing house to include an oratory. He also inherited three fourths of the lordship of the manor, and at last for a short time Dorking had resident lords; Howard at Deepdene and Sir Ambrose Browne at Betchworth Castle.

Law and Order

Manor courts, now held on average no more than twice a year, were devoted to estate business. Civil matters such as highway maintenance, bastardy orders, trading regulations and licensing were either dealt with by the Vestry, or went before the Quarter Sessions, which now were held sometimes in Dorking, perhaps in the market house, which also accommodated a cage or prison cell.

On seven occasions between 1625 and 1669 the County Assizes were also held in the town and those found guilty of capital offences were hanged on the gallows at Sandy Cross, at what is now the corner of Coldharbour Lane and Ridgeway Road. Most were afterwards buried in St. Martin's churchyard, but according to the parish register none was from Dorking. This does not imply of course that Dorking was a particularly law-abiding town, merely that its transgressors were tried at Assizes held elsewhere.

An expanding town

The Hearth Tax returns for 1664 record the number of households in the parish as 352, and it can be estimated that in spite of several severe outbreaks of plague the population had risen to approximately 1,600. An increasing cause for concern at the manor court was the number of encroachments on common land like Cotmandene and the Holmwood, where over-crowding in the town centre was driving people to build new cottages.

In the town centre larger and more prestigious houses were being built and as a glance at The Old Vicarage at the northern corner of Vincent's Lane, or at 77 South Street (Little Dudley House) will confirm, brick-making and bricklaying had become major trades. Horticulture and ornamental gardens were also becoming fashionable. Many crofts were turned into orchards, and in 1683 a gardener called Robert Newman had a nursery in Dene Street at the corner of Cotmandene. This may be the same Master Newman who showed John Aubrey round the newly laid-out grounds of the Deepdene in 1673.

Little Dudley House, 77 South Street. *Undated lithograph. (Surrey Archaeological Society).*

Caves under 125-127 High Street, formerly the Sun Public House. *Photograph dated 1970. (Surrey County Council).*

Underground Dorking

Exploitation of the underlying sandy rock now started on a large scale, leaving caverns under many of the houses in the town, which were then utilised as cellars. The most spectacular of these can be seen in South Street, where the owner designed a complex of carefully architected compartments and stairs leading to a circular chamber 50 feet below. Other interesting, though probably later, developments lie under the White Horse Hotel, and at 125–127 High Street where there are two rectangular rooms with arched roofs, rather reminiscent of Nissen huts, which were used for meetings of the otherwise unrecorded Sparrow Club in the 19th century. Below 39 High Street, formerly the Wheatsheaf public house, there are many stairs and passages and a circular cock-fighting pit.

Aubrey passes by

. . . no where are finer Caves for the Preservation of their Liquor than in the Sand here . . .

This observation was made by John Aubrey in a description of the town included in his *Natural History and Antiquities of Surrey,* written in about 1673. Unfortunately the book was not published until after his death and his editor confused some of his notes on Dorking, Capel and Reigate, resulting in a few inaccuracies. In the main, however, Aubrey presented a valuable contemporary record. Amongst other details, he confirmed that there was still a fair at Ascension but that the market day was then only once a week, on Thursday, and that it was chiefly for corn and fat poultry. In fact he claimed that it was the greatest market for poultry in England, and he was of course referring to the unusual breed of five-clawed fowls called Dorkings which were nationally famous for their qualities as table birds. Sadly, he was less impressed by the townswomen, and compared them and the local cattle unfavourably with those of other counties. He did add that the air was incomparably sweet on Cotmandene, but that the roads to the south were impassable after only a little rain.

Aubrey probably journeyed during the summer months on horseback and could avoid the worst conditions on the roads, but others needed to travel to and from Dorking at all times of year and in all weathers. The gentry owned coaches, wagons delivered timber to the wharves at Kingston, and corn and animals from the outlying areas were vital to the market. For all these, the unmetalled roads, particularly through the heavy clay to the south, but also on the slippery chalk of the North Downs, presented a problem which was not be resolved satisfactorily until the next century.

This panorama of Dorking, painted c. 1780, shows two-stump cricket being played on Cotmandene. The scene is dominated by Charles Howard's recently completed Palladian Mansion at Deepdene, with the stable block on the left and the dene rising to the temple. At the bottom left, London Road runs between Pippbrook Mill and Pippbrook House and its stables. On the right is the medieval church, with Butter Hill House visible to its right. To the left of the church, along the line of the High Street, the upper parts of the Red Lion, the Dutch House, and the White Horse can be seen. Below Cotmandene lies Shrub Hill, with its grounds running down to the Pippbrook, while in the foreground are the mill ponds. *Oil Painting attributed to James Canter. (Marylebone Cricket Club).*

CHAPTER FIVE

THE LONG EIGHTEENTH CENTURY: 1689–1836

Brian Overell

Old, ill-lit and badly paved

Dorking's story during the 18th century is one of progressive loss of its old identity, but the beginning of discovery of a new. Until the fourth quarter of the century, the story was one of decline. In 1787 the *Gentleman's Magazine* described Dorking, with a population of 1,800, as 'old, ill-lit and badly paved'.

Dorking was buried in the country; it was not on a good road. Although it can be seen on the map to occupy a key position at the junction of north-south and east-west lines of communication, these lines had been so neglected that in winter they barely existed. The Roman Stane Street to the south had long been abandoned from where it leaves the current Horsham Road at North Holmwood and skirts the Redland Hills until it appears, again as a maintained road, towards and through Ockley. Daniel Defoe said of Stane Street in Dorking in 1724 ' . . . we see little of it now: and the country indeed remains in the utmost distress for want of good roads. So over the whole Wild [Weald] of Kent and Sussex it is the same, where the corn is cheap at the barn because it cannot be carried out, and dear in the market because it cannot be brought in'.

Since Saxon times, Dorking's route south had been via Coldharbour Lane, which leaves the Horsham Road at the southern end of South Street; at Coldharbour the road branches steeply down to meet Stane Street again towards Ockley. Coldharbour Lane is now in part a picturesque drive between deep banks furrowed out in the soft greensand: the conditions which caused this furrowing before the road was metalled were clearly appalling. A possibly apochryphal story is that the road was so narrow that coffin bearers had to walk in single file. Perhaps such sepulchral stories about this road were encouraged by its passing over Gallows Hill. The precise course of the road sometimes changed as the old one became more impassable; in parts an old track is still identifiable next to the current one.

To the north, the exact route of Stane Street had also been lost. London-bound traffic could cross the Mole at Burford and climb the Mickleham Downs; or, especially in winter, take the Reigate road to a point where, opposite the current entrance to Betchworth Golf Club, it could cross the river before hauling up to the top. (The last road bridge here was washed away in the flood of 1968, and was replaced by a footbridge).

Travelling conditions in winter were atrocious. Surrey roads were said to be the worst in England, and even as late as 1805 were compared with those in some of the most inaccessible and uninhabited parts of Ireland. About 1750 Dr. John Burton, going from Kingston to Ockley, abandoned his coach at Epsom and continued on horseback: by no other means could he get across the Downs. The Wealden clay became impassable; south of Dorking, residents of Horsham claimed conditions to be so bad that their quickest route to London was via Canterbury in Kent.

So although Dorking nominally stood on a main road from London to the coast, it was not a flourishing crossroads, but a small market town, its size limited by its catchment area, and by the practicalities of transport to London.

Its situation can be contrasted with that of Guildford, which had solved some of its communications problems. This was the period when the national canal system was being developed, and by 1653 Guildford was in direct communication with the Thames and London via the Wey Navigation. As a result, Guildford rather than Dorking grew as a central distribution point for beer, paper, timber and agricultural produce generally, much of which went to London. The timber was brought in summer from over 30 miles away in Sussex and Hampshire. Much of the excellent timber around Dorking, however, for instance in the Holmwood and in Ashcombe Wood, was uncullable because of the lack of accessible markets. It was commonplace in Surrey to see timber abandoned in mid-journey by the wayside, wherever winter overtook it, awaiting summer for continuation of a journey which, if directed towards distant shipyards, could take several years. Dorking's timber would usually be taken to Thames Ditton, where it was transferred to barges.

Dorking might have become part of a canal network, since a number of plans were made. In 1664 an Act was granted to make the Mole navigable from near Reigate to the Thames, but this was never executed. A later scheme, put forward in 1798, advocated the connection of the Arun Canal to Horsham, thence to the chalk pits at Betchworth, and down the Mole valley to the market at Dorking, while in 1810 proposals for a Grand Southern Canal from the Medway to Portsmouth included a Thames connection via the Mole valley. None of these schemes was implemented.

The decline of the town in the latter part of the 18th century is perhaps symbolised by the decay of the market house. This stood in the road west of the White Horse, rather as the surviving market house in Reigate still does today; it contained the town jail and the civic offices in the upper storey. In a ruinous state, it was criticised for being an eyesore, for blocking the road, and for obstructing the view of Box Hill. It was pulled down, there being an understanding with the Duke of Norfolk, who had by that time bought the remaining fourth of the Manor, that he would see to its rebuilding. But the Duke died, and the undertaking was not honoured. Eventually agreement was reached that proceeds from the sale of demolition materials should help defray the costs of paving and lighting the town in 1817–18.

The Coming of the Turnpike Road: Catching up with the Romans

Financed by the Turnpike system, a major road building programme commenced in the middle of the century, and in 1755 Horsham got its shorter route to London via Dorking. From Leatherhead the road followed the River Mole south to Mickleham, where it bore left to the Fox and Hounds Inn, now the Burford Bridge Hotel, at the foot of Box Hill. A new bridge was built at this time, and the road crossed to the Cock Inn at Giles Green where there was the Dorking tollgate and a milestone: 8 miles from Epsom, 5 furlongs to Dorking: then over the Pippbrook, a new bridge being built in 1786. Turning right, with the first Pippbrook House on its left, it continued up what is still the London Road to the east end of the High Street. There was a smithy at the corner of the Reigate Road on the left, while the road turned right into Dorking.

South out of Dorking, the road passed up South Street to the Queen's Head Inn to turn sharply left at a blacksmith's shop into what is now the

Painted about 1840, John Beckett's picture shows the Turnpike Road leaving Dorking at the southern end of the town by the Queen's Head. It continued through 'The Hollows' where it had been raised and levelled earlier in the century. *(Dorking Museum)*.

Horsham Road, and then to run between high banks in a stretch known as 'The Hollows'. In the first part of the 19th century, the level of this part of the road was raised, and the bank to the east was cut back to make the present raised pathway: at the same time, the turning at the Queen's Head was improved. The toll gate, known as 'Harrow Gate', was situated at the junction with Hampstead Road, with a blacksmith's on the opposite corner. Later, in 1857, as the tide of house building flowed out of town, the gate was to be moved to a site further south, just past the Bush Inn; the tollkeeper's cottage was then on the right of the south side of the gate, with a pedestrian gate on the path to the left. Over the hill, and opposite to the Windmill Inn, there was a rope-maker's walk, which survived into the present century. This piece of land, still apparent between the road and the hedge, now serves as an unofficial car park for local residents.

Crossing the Bentsbrook to Holmwood common, the road originally climbed the hill past where the church now stands; the then estate of Chart Park could be seen to the east from this vantage point. This part of the route still exists as a wide footpath. It descended to Mid-Holmwood past an inn, the Nag's Head, which is now a private house. In the first part of the last century, when the current route up Spook Hill replaced the difficult climb over the Common, the business of the Nag's Head was transferred to the Norfolk Arms over the road, which also remains today as a private house. With a further gate at Holmwood corner, the road continued along the route of what was to become the A24 to Horsham.

A further turnpike road was built from Horsham to Steyning via Partridge Green in 1764. This provided Dorking with a connection with Brighton, but no good connection with Worthing was established until an Act of 1802 authorised construction of the road from West Grinstead via Dial Post and Findon, and thus completed the route of the present A24.

The east-west road through Dorking remained as a parish-maintained road, and as such did little to help Dorking share in Guildford's canal-borne prosperity. Efforts were made in around 1830 to improve Coast Hill; the difficulties it posed were made good use of by highwaymen. There was a tollbar on this road in West Street, taking 2½d. toll on each taxable vehicle. On the eastern side of the town, the still-existing road crosses Boxhill bridge and then turns right to pass south of the modern A25 road to go to Betchworth before rejoining the present main route at Buckland.

Markets

With the coming of the turnpike road, Dorking could reasonably hope for an increase in trade and prosperity. It already had a fair trade in its corn market, which had grown from the 17th century. The market

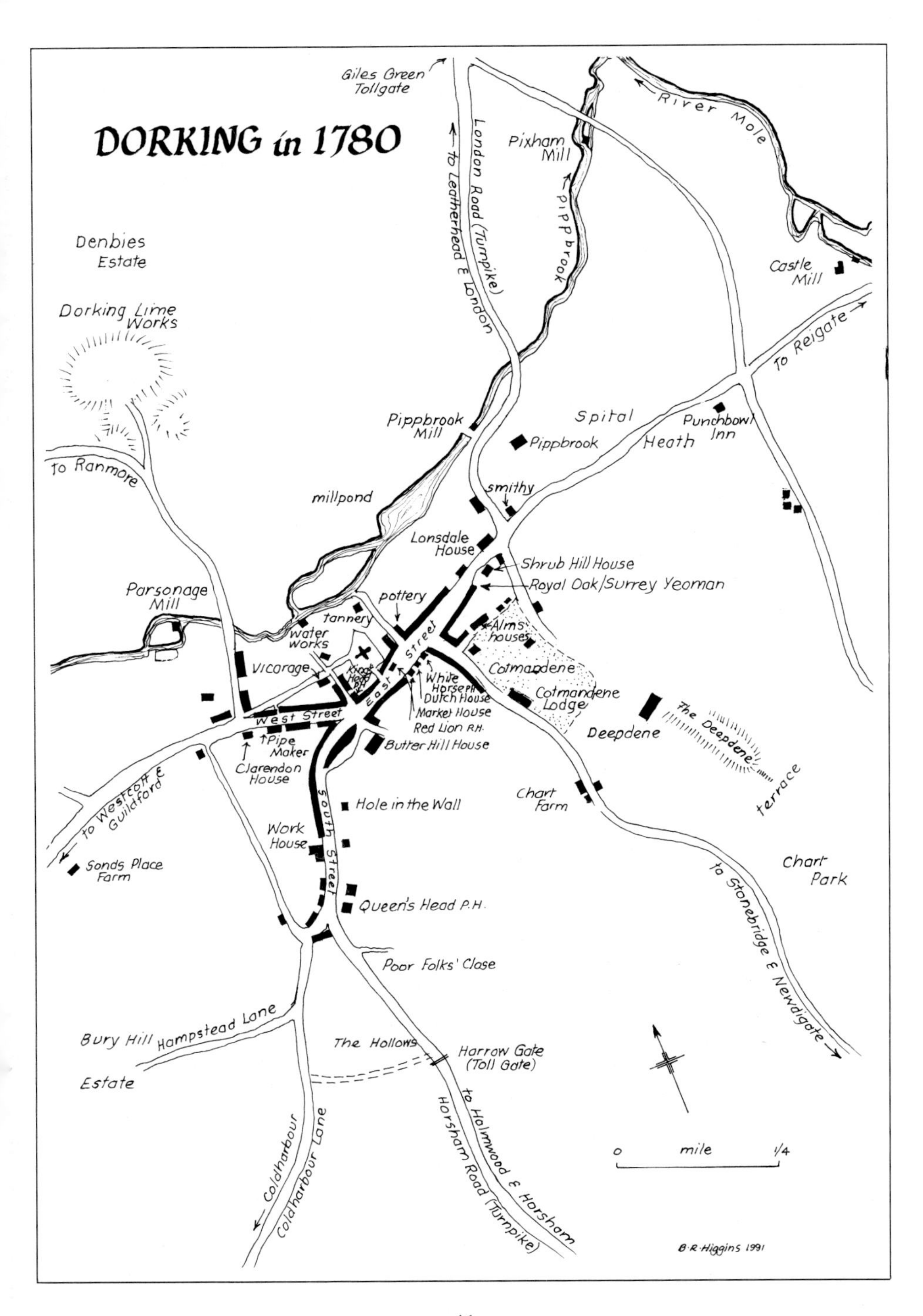
DORKING in 1780
Giles Green Tollgate
to Leatherhead & London
London Road (Turnpike)
Pixham Mill
Pippbrook
River Mole
Castle Mill
Denbies Estate
Dorking Lime Works
to Reigate
Spital Heath
Punchbowl Inn
Pippbrook Mill
Pippbrook
To Ranmore
smithy
millpond
Lonsdale House
Shrub Hill House
Royal Oak/Surrey Yeoman
Parsonage Mill
pottery
Tannery
water works
Alms houses
Vicarage
East Street
White Horse PH
Dutch House
Market House
Red Lion P.H.
Cotmandene
Cotmandene Lodge
Deepdene
The Deepdene
West Street
Pipe Maker
Butter Hill House
Clarendon House
to Westcott & Guildford
Hole in the Wall
Chart Farm
terrace
Work House
South Street
Sonds Place Farm
Chart Park
Queen's Head P.H.
to Stonebridge & Newdigate
Poor Folks' Close
Bury Hill Estate
Hampstead Lane
The Hollows
Harrow Gate (Toll Gate)
Coldharbour
Coldharbour Lane
Horsham Road (Turnpike)
to Holmwood & Horsham
0 mile 1/4
B.R.Higgins 1991

was held on Thursdays, but market tolls were often avoided by doing the deals in public houses which specialised in providing the service; the Three Tuns and Black Horse Inns were both on the north side of the High Street, but are now demolished. Corn was pitched onto the floor to be assessed for quality. Sussex corn was valued more than the local product, weighing more per sack, but 10s. per load was charged for its carriage from Horsham.

The hoped-for increase in trade did in fact occur, but not for long. Improvements in other roads, such as the Reigate to Povey Cross road, one of the first turnpikes to have been built, opened up alternative routes for Horsham to connect with London. Horsham became the more convenient centre for Sussex trade, and Dorking found its own trade diminishing.

Nevertheless, a substantial poultry market continued on into the present century, specialising particularly in five-clawed Dorking hens; fattening of these hens to 4–6lb apiece by farmers' wives was a substantial cottage industry. Higglers would purchase birds for packing and for onward distribution. Daniel Defoe observed that the Dorking capon was well-known to poulterers in London's Leadenhall Market: while in the mid-19th century, Edward Lear made a poetical reference to the Dorking hen in 'The Courtship of the Yonghy-Bonghy-Bo' ' . . . he heard a lady talking, to some milk-white hens of Dorking . . .'

In the first half of the 18th century, the ancient livestock market held on Ascension Eve filled the High Street from end to end with cattle on the south side; and from outside the Red Lion eastwards on the north side with sheep and pigs. For lambs, it was one of the greatest fairs in England but, like the corn market, it declined in the second half of the century when Horsham farmers could send their lambs direct to London via Reigate. On Ascension day, the fair devoted itself to sale of other goods, and to pleasure.

Lime for London

Dorking was very dependent on agriculture for much of its trade; in the absence of good transport one of its biggest assets, the lime made from the chalk of the North Downs, also had a largely agricultural market. Sometimes the chalk would be taken away by farmers and burnt on the farms. But this business prospered with better transport to London, and in 1805 Dorking was said to have the best chalkpits in the county, if not in England. The pits, which are no longer worked, can be found up Chalkpit Lane at the foot of Ranmore Road on the north of the town. Here were several large kilns for making the lime, which was of such quality that it was eagerly sought by masons and bricklayers in

London. The Dorking product was used extensively in building the second Somerset House and the Bank of England in the late 18th century. Especially valued for its property of hardening under water, it proved invaluable in construction of both the West India (1802) and the London (1805) docks. Following the road improvements, it was taken by teams direct to London, or to Kingston and thence by barges on the Thames. Coal would be carried on the return journey both for kiln firing and for sale, so that every lime merchant was also a coal merchant. Other works were opened in the late 18th and early 19th century at Brockham, and at Betchworth, where the Dorking Greystone Lime Company associated itself by inference with the famous Dorking lime.

A Limekiln in the chalkpits near Dorking. Engraving dated 1802. *(Surrey Archaeological Society).*

Production of other building materials, bricks and sand, was widespread, but generally in small scale operations until the 19th century. The building industry was then, as now, prone to cycles of boom and depression. In 1823 the lime trade started to climb out of depression, which itself had followed a boom, due to what was described as 'London building mania'.

Pottery, Tanning and Clay Pipes

Within the town there is evidence of a pottery on the east side of Mill Lane; it had probably closed by the 19th century. Fragments discovered on the site are now in Guildford Museum.

A pottery in Chart Lane was said to make pipes for the conveyance of water which were superior to the wooden or leaden pipes then generally used. An inch and a quarter in diameter, they were laid at an inclusive cost of 13d. per yard. On the west side of Mill Lane, down by the brook, there was a tannery. It was said that workers there did not become infected during smallpox epidemics, no doubt, like dairy farm workers, they became immune through exposure to cowpox. (In the 1760s Dorking surgeons were carrying out vaccination with live smallpox; one effect seems to have been to increase the rates of infection in the town, and the Vestry eventually banned this practice).

The end of Mill Lane, viewed across the Pippbrook c. 1840. *Photograph of oil painting by John Beckett. (Dorking Museum)*

In West Street there was a maker of clay pipes on the site of what was later the Public Hall. George Thornton's pipehouse and yard comprised, when he died in 1769, three tenements with outhouses, pipe-shop, yard and garden to the value of £400.

Another West Street industry established in the 1820s was the Iron Foundry, developed on part of the Queen's Arms site at the east end of the street by John Bartlett, blacksmith, and his son George. In 1881 it was taken over by Walter Stone and Henry Edward Turner.

Brewing

In the 1840s the tannery in Mill Lane was replaced by Boxall's brewery; the presence of a spring here may have influenced the choice of site. Another brewery, Cheesman's, in South Street, south of where the Spotted Dog now stands, was operational early in the 19th century. Before this one had operated in the King's Head yard. By the mid-19th century, Young's in Church Street, Lucock's on the south side of High Street, and the Red Lion Brewery, all added to the fragrance of Dorking air. These were relatively small operations, and were all swept away in the later 19th century by the rise of the big brewers.

Nursing the Foundlings

A source of employment for women was the wet nursing of illegitimate pauper babies sent to Dorking and other Surrey and Kent locations from the Foundling Hospital in London. The custom from 1760 was to lodge them with their country foster parents until they were four or five years old; they were then brought back to the Hospital to be educated. But for many of the infants it came too late; of 63 interments in Dorking churchyard recorded in 1769, 20 were of foundlings.

Watermills and Waterworks

Dorking had two watermills operational during the 18th century, though others were close by at the Westcott Rookery and at Milton Court to the west, and at Pixham and at Betchworth to the east.

Parsonage Mill was on the Pippbrook at the west end of Dorking, on what is now the Curtis Road industrial estate. The last water mill, built there in 1702, as evidenced by a fire mark, survived until 1959, by which time two and a half centuries of random repairs and additions had given it an appearance of unique charm. A leat from the Pippbrook fed a pond, which drove an overshot waterwheel. For the greater part of its life, beginning in 1788, it was operated by the corn merchants, Attlee's.

Pippbrook Mill, variously known as Patching Mill or Dorking Mill, occupied an 11th century site, and its millpond is shown on the 1649 Manorial Survey map. The last working mill here dated from the end of the 18th century. It was a powerful mill, with the spillway going through the centre of the mill building to drive the machinery of the southern half; the northern half was powered by an overshot waterwheel.

At the end of North Street is a continuation, which runs down to the Pippbrook. Here in 1735 was founded the first Dorking waterworks:

HORSHAM and DORKING
Turnpike Road.

CONTRACT

FOR

Providing & conveying Materials for the repair of the said road

THE TRUSTEES

WILL AT A MEETING TO BE HELD

On MONDAY the 29th. of AUGUST, 1836,

At the RED LION INN, DORKING,

Receive Tenders from such Persons as may be willing to Contract for the supply and for the delivery of the following Materials on the undermentioned Divisions of the Road for the repairs thereof, for one year commencing on the said 29th. day of AUGUST next.

THE FOLLOWING LENGTHS

TO BE REPAIRED WITH SURFACE PICKED FLINTS,

To be Provided, Broken and Conveyed to and on the

1st. Division.—Commencing at the Watch House in Epsom and ending at the Hatch Gate in Ashtead, ... 1½ Miles.

2nd. Division.—Commencing at the Hatch Gate in Ashtead, and ending at the 18th. Mile Post in Leatherhead Common Fields, ... 2 Miles.

3rd. Division.—Commencing at the 18th. Mile Post, and ending at the 19th. Mile Post, near Vale Lodge,... .... 1 Mile.

4th. Division.—Commencing at the 19th. Mile Post, and ending at the 21st. Mile Post, near Juniper Hall, ... 2 Miles.

The Following Lengths to be repaired with Flint

From the Pit at Gyles Green in Dorking, and to be Carted to and on the

5th. Division.—Commencing at the 21st. Mile Post, and ending at the 23rd. Mile Post, near Mr. Westland's Nursery,........ 2 Miles.

6th. Division.—Commencing at the 23rd. Mile Post, and ending at the 24th. Mile Post, near the Harrow Turnpike Gate,........ 1 Mile.

7th. Division.—Commencing at the 24th. Mile Post, and ending at the 26th Mile Post, near the Watering Pond on the Holmwood,........ 2 Miles.

The above Materials are to be brought on the Road in Carriages with Wheels not less than 6 inches in breadth, and to be Carted and laid on the Road according to the directions of the Surveyor to the Trustees.—by order of the Trustees,

JAMES WHITE,
SURVEYOR.

The Tenders for the first Four Divisions are to be for broken Flints, at per Cubic Yard, so that they shall pass through a sieve the mesh of which shall not exceed 2 inches, and a separate Price for each Division, on the first Four Divisions and also for the Carting on each of the remaining Divisions.

Dorking, August 1st. 1836.

R. B. EDE, PRINTER, DORKING.

a commemorative plaque is attached to the old works building, Brookside. Nearby the old water works cottages are still standing as Nos. 3 and 4 Archway Place, but now carry later additions. The water, obtained from a spring lying close to the brook, was distributed in wooden pipes made from bored tree trunks. In 1739, and again in 1740, the Vestry authorised expenditure for a water engine, probably a pump powered by the brook. The waterworks founder, Resta Patching Jr., the son of a prominent Quaker in the town, became bankrupt and was imprisoned in the Fleet in 1743 for falsification of accounts. The works did not satisfy all requirements: in 1780 the Vestry agreed to reopen a well of water "in the grounds of John Eagles" and erect a pump — possibly the one at Pump Corner. Nevertheless, the works survived, and in 1829 was offering showerbaths at 1s. per bath. But by the mid-19th century the spring had become contaminated by the brook, which was by then grossly polluted with sewage, and this source was closed down.

Postal Services and Stage Coaches

The new turnpike road brought an improvement in the postal services. The mail coach left Dorking for London every evening except Saturday, and returned during the same night. A letter from London cost 6d., collected from the recipient. The mail man carried pistols, showing that the threat of highway robbery was real, not an imagined or romanticised fiction. He was not allowed to collect the new mail bags until he had demonstrated to the official at the Post Office, then situated opposite the Wheatsheaf Inn in the High Street, that the pistols were loaded. Guns were also carried by commercial vehicles using the turnpike; crossing Holmwood common, a haunt of vagrants, thieves and highwaymen, was no picnic.

The arrival of the railway in 1849 brought the stage coach era to a close, except as a tourist amusement, but until that date there was a steadily improving service. Initially, coaches would set out on one day to London, returning on the next, but eventually the journey time was reduced to 3–4 hours in summer, an average speed of 8 mph; winter times could be much longer. In 1787 the coach from the King's Head arrived at the Spreadeagle in Gracechurch Street at 11 a.m. in summer, at 3 p.m. in winter; it returned the same day at 3 p.m. in summer, but stayed overnight until 8 o'clock next morning in winter.

Dorking's most famous coachman was William Broad, who died in 1862. He lived close to the Bull's Head in South Street, from where his London coach started every day at 7 a.m., returning in the evening. Walker's coach started from the same inn at 3 p.m., returning the following day. In 1837, four local coaches served London daily. Others came through from elsewhere: 16 coaches and two post wagons travelled through Holmwood every day on the Dorking to Horsham turnpike.

In addition to coaches, post chaise horses could be hired at the White Horse and at the King's Head.

This was not cheap travel available to everyone. Walker's coach, for instance, charged half a guinea (10s 6d) for the journey to London; £55 might be a reasonable estimate at today's values. Cheaper but slower travel was, of course, available. The 'Haggle* Vann' left for Gracechurch Street twice a week for a fare of 2s 6d, even so, no trivial sum. Travel was for the affluent classes, and they showed their appreciation of the service by coming to live in Dorking. The turnpike road produced the anticipated upturn in Dorking's fortunes, not by increasing agricultural trade, but by bringing new money into the town. The parish register started to record large numbers of military, naval and titled folk. New houses were built; old houses were renovated and extended; and great estates developed around the town, processes which were in due course to be accelerated by the coming of the railways.

The Estates of the Prosperous

One of the big estates, already developing in the 17th century, was the Deepdene, or Dibden, situated on the south east side of Dorking town. By 1664 a substantial new house, with 18 fire hearths, had been built there by the Hon. Charles Howard, who had inherited the estate with three-fourths of the manor of Dorking in 1652. Making imaginative use of the natural hollow of the hill, the 'dene', he laid out extensive gardens which received high praise first from John Evelyn and then from John Aubrey, who has left us a detailed description of them as well as a sketch of the lay-out. Howard also built a laboratory in the steep side of the dene where he studied chemistry and applied his scientific knowledge to a number of practical matters such as leather tanning and the cultivation of saffron. He continued to live at the Deepdene until his death in 1713 at the age of 83. He was buried in St. Martin's church alongside his wife Mary, who had died in 1696. His son and heir, Henry Charles Howard, survived him by only seven years and he too was buried at Dorking, his widow living on until 1747. Their son, another Charles, also came to live at Deepdene and by 1768 was building a 'very handsome' house in late Palladian style, which was substantially complete in 1775. Building accounts survive identifying a number of local brickmakers, bricklayers and other tradesmen engaged in this work.

On the death of his second cousin in 1777, Charles became the 10th Duke of Norfolk, but he and his duchess Katherine continued to spend their summers at the Deepdene. He died in 1786 and was buried in Dorking.

---

* 'Haggle' probably in the obsolete sense of 'proceeding slowly or with difficulty', rather than the modern meaning of bargaining over the fare.

Their son, the 11th Duke, sold the Deepdene in 1790, buying an estate at Newdigate, but not living to see the completion of the mansion he began building there, which was never finished. He also began the restoration of Arundel Castle. He continued the Howard tradition of being a promoter of arts and sciences, generously lending the Deepdene to the dramatist, Sheridan, (later owner of Polesden Lacey) for some time before selling it. The Duke, however, broke with the Howard tradition of Roman Catholicism, becoming an Anglican shortly before his election as M.P. for Carlisle in 1780; nine years later he purchased the patronage of Dorking Church and in 1797 bought the last quarter of the Manor. As a person, though generous and in many ways public spirited, he was gross and slovenly and a heavy drinker, disliking soap and water so much, it is said, that his servants could only wash him when he was in a drunken stupor. The "Protestant Duke" died in 1815 and was the last of the Howards to be buried in Dorking. The ceremony was effected with all the honour due to him as premier Duke and hereditary Earl Marshal of England. His remains, brought from his London residence, Norfolk House, to Burford Bridge, were joined there by a splendidly accoutred cavalcade of kings of arms, heralds, nobility and gentlemen with their attendants, such as Dorking had seldom, if ever, seen. The procession was met at St. Martin's church gate at 5 p.m. by the vicar of Dorking, who performed the exequies in a church crammed to capacity. The stone slab, which formerly covered the Duke's resting place, now lies somewhat defaced, outside the south wall of the church.

Sir William Burrell, Bart., who had purchased the estate from the Duke, died in 1796, his widow surviving until 1802. Deepdene was again up for sale in 1807, when the sales catalogue gave a detailed description. The 'modern brick-built house' had four principal rooms on the ground floor designated library, dining, breakfast and billiard rooms. The drawing room on the first floor had a commanding view of the countryside. There were four bedrooms on this floor, five in the upper storey, and one on the ground floor. The basement held the domestic offices, and there was a 'noble kitchen'. The gardens included walks, 'rural retirements', grottoes, caverns, a terrace, a 'canal of water' and hothouses.

The next purchaser, in 1808, was Thomas Hope (1764–1831), a collector of antique sculptures and works of art, who became a recognised arbiter of taste for neo-classical architecture and decoration. He enlarged and enhanced the house to include a new library, a new dining room, two orangeries and a conservatory, and a gallery to house his collection of sculptures. He also extended the estate and built new carriageways and lodges. In 1833 the result was described as the finest example in England of an Italianate villa.

When Thomas Hope died, he was interred in the grounds in a mausoleum, which already contained the remains of his young son,

Charles. This building still exists, but is now sealed and buried to roof level. His son, Henry Thomas Hope (1808–62), continued to enlarge and improve the estate until by 1838 it had a circumference of 12 miles, extending north over Box Hill, and east past Brockham. Henry also enhanced and extended the mansion, converting it to a 'sumptuous High Renaissance palazzo'.

This view of Deepdene House shows Thomas Hope's Italianate villa in 1828. *Engraving by G. F. Prosser from 'Select illustrations of the County of Surrey . . . ' (Surrey Archaeological Society).*

Defoe had noted that good wine was produced from the Howard estate. In 1710 it was recorded that 'there is in the parish a vineyard belonging to Lord Howard with a wine press and other necessary materials, where several hogsheads of wine have been made in many years'. The vineyard was on a piece of ground known as Bridehills lying to the south of Deepdene estate. Over the hill was a villa known as the Vintage House with a cottage which was eventually turned into stables. Henry Howard sold his property in 1718, and in 1746 it was purchased by a merchant, Henry Talbot, who had become wealthy from the proceeds of several voyages to China with the East India Company. From 1735 onwards he held a post as one of the commissioners for collecting duty on salt, worth £500 p.a. Soon afterwards, on the death of Henry Howard's widow, he acquired the lease of the Howard estate, which he kept until 1767, when Charles Howard resumed occupation. Henry Talbot bought other surrounding properties known as Chart, creating Chart Park, much of it over the land now occupied by Dorking Golf Club, and made a hanging garden on the side of the hill. Chart Park was eventually incorporated into the Deepdene estate in 1813–14, when it was purchased for £30,000 and presented to Thomas Hope by his brother, a most generous gift, which Thomas commemorated by building a temple on the Deepdene terrace inscribed FRATRI OPTVMO H.P.H.

The terrace is still open to the public, although neglect and vandalism led to demolition of the temple in 1955. Thomas Hope demolished the house at Chart Park, and no picture of it has been identified. He was also responsible for demolishing much of Betchworth Castle when he acquired its estate, and a villa which occupied the site of the present Deepdene Gardens.

On the opposite side of Dorking, on Ranmore Common, another great house, Denbies, arose during this period. Jonathan Tyers, the proprietor of Vauxhall Pleasure Gardens, purchased Denbies farm in 1734, proceeding to develop it as a country seat. However, perhaps in compensation for the way in which he made his money, he imparted a peculiarly solemn character to the house and grounds, with everything designed to direct the mind to serious thoughts. A wood about eight acres in extent, in the centre of which a small temple was erected, profuse with inscriptions designed to induce reflections of a most serious nature, was named 'Il Penseroso' after Milton's poem. Here a clock struck at the end of every minute, reminding the visitor of the passing of time: two life-size figures, representing respectively Christian and Unbeliever in their last moments, were drawn to his attention by a figure of Truth trampling on a mask; and a lady's and a gentleman's skull respectively surmounted poems which included such lines as 'I, once, was lovely, and belov'd – like you', and 'Yet know – I feasted but to feast a worm'.

Despite these apparent concerns with the deeper side of life, Tyers did not show much sympathy to the interests of the Rev. Phillip Walton, Vicar of Dorking and Rector of Mickleham. In 1747 Tyers, who had grown about six acres of hops on the estate, refused to deliver the vicar's tithe, telling him to pick it himself; every tenth hill, comprising four lines of six squares, was left for him unpicked. In the subsequent court action, Tyers lost; it was judged that crops were not titheable until picked. Tyers vindictively proceeded to grub up the hops. After his death in 1767, the next purchaser, Peter King, saw to it that the 'grave conceits' in the wood were expunged.

In 1787 the property was purchased by Joseph Denison, son of a self-made merchant and banker. He was noted locally for retaining the common touch, addressing a Dorking tradesman by his Christian name, and carrying home himself a leg of mutton whenever he came into Dorking, apparently to commemorate the first dinner he had when he arrived in London. His son, William Joseph Denison, inherited the property in 1806, extending the estate and, as M.P. for West Surrey. becoming a well-known public figure and local benefactor. A plaque of the Denison arms was later found on the site of the demolished old house, and may now be seen on the wall on the town side of the Cotmandene flats.

One other big estate lying close to Dorking, but on the west side, was Bury Hill, which lay on Milton Street up the Westcott Road. Like Denbies, it was purchased as a farm, Chadhurst Farm, by a rich man, Edward Walter, who built the mansion. He added to the estate, and on his death in 1780 it passed to his daughter, Harriot, whose husband, Viscount Grimston, was in 1815 created Baron Verulam. In 1805 the estate was acquired by the Barclays, the family of Southwark brewers. The estate, which is characterised by a large ornamental lake, bordered on Coldharbour Lane.

The 18th Century Town

At the east end of town, where the Dorking public library now occupies a later house, the first Pippbrook mansion was built in the 1750s by William Page, who occupied it until 1764. It was described as a 'neat brick building with winged offices which projected forward and were joined to the house by circular colonnades'.

At the east end of the High Street was a public house known as the Royal Oak. Next to it lay the house which had once belonged to Lawrence Marsh, and which came to be called Shrub Hill. Some remnants remain:

Shrub Hill was formerly occupied by Lawrence Marsh. *Watercolour by Edward Hassell dated 1830. (Surrey Archaeological Society).*

a bay window can be seen in the alley leading to the Strict Baptist Chapel. The property passed through a number of distinguished hands during this century, but is now mainly remembered for its occupancy by the Leslie family. It was purchased in 1792 by Baron Leslie, who succeeded in 1810 to the title of Earl of Rothes. It was in his honour, as Colonel of the Surrey Yeomanry, that the public house adjoining the grounds, the Royal Oak, became the Surrey Yeoman, the name under which it operates today. In 1816, George III's Queen Charlotte stopped at Shrub Hill on a journey from Brighton to Windsor, and took breakfast. She is said to have left six eggs untouched, and they were gilded as a memento. The Earl died in 1817, after collapsing while going to hunt in Betchworth Park. Although he had taken his mother's name of Leslie, his father had been an Evelyn, and the Earl was buried in the Evelyn's church at Wotton, where a plaque marks the place. The Dowager Countess continued in residence for many years with her two daughters, Mary and Elizabeth Jane; the title passed to the Earl's daughter by a previous marriage.

Lady Elizabeth Jane married Captain Augustus Wathen of the 15th Lancers, a veteran of Waterloo. Wathen endured a famous one month's court martial at the end of 1833 after falling foul of his regimental colonel, Lord James Brudenell, who was later to achieve greater fame after succeeding to the title of 7th Earl of Cardigan and leading the charge of the Light Brigade in the Crimean War. The charges against Captain Wathen were found to be not merely groundless, but malicious, and as a result Lord Brudenell lost his colonelcy. On his return to Dorking, Wathen had his carriage drawn in triumph through the streets by the inhabitants, preceded by the town band. Rothes and Wathen are commemorated in the names of the roads in the Victorian estate built on the north side of the High Street, where the Shrub Hill coach-house, stables, meadow and kitchen garden lay; and Pixham has a Leslie road.

The Dutch House. *Engraving from J. Timbs' 'A Picturesque Promenade Around Dorking', published in 1823.*

In the middle of the town, adjoining the White Horse on the west side, there is a large, but now undistinguished, building; records show that a house had been there since 1585. Following the fashion for all things Dutch, which came with William of Orange, it was rebuilt in the Dutch style. Pictures reveal that it had a central doorway approached by a flight of steps, and bay windows on each side surmounted by rounded Dutch pediments. Following its sale in 1820, it was converted into three houses and, eventually, in the late 19th century, into shops, one of which is now incorporated into the White Horse. During this process, it lost its frontage, and the coach entrance on the right was driven through where there was previously a side door.

Round the corner, in South Street, Butter Hill House, which originally included the adjoining Rose Hill House, was rebuilt early in the 18th century; it has Victorian additions which include the picturesque archway. The path under the archway was then the private approach to the rear, and not a public way. The area behind, known as 'Bottom field', or colloquially as 'Back Field', contained no other houses. Louis-Philippe, King of France 1830–48, was said to have spent some childhood years here during the period of Revolution, when a small colony of French aristocrats also settled at nearby Mickleham, but there is no confirmation of this. At this time Fanny Burney, who married the emigré General d'Arblay, paid a visit with him to Dr. John Aitkin MD at his lodgings in Dorking, where he was spending the summer with his family 'on account of his ill-health, the air of the town having been recommended for his complaints'. The Butter Hill estate was sold in 1831, and the house divided into two.

At the far end of West Street, Clarendon House was largely rebuilt during the 18th century by Resta Patching Sr., father of the founder of the waterworks. Some of the earlier work remained; in the 1980s it was saved from demolition and again rebuilt, retaining its original frontage.

Some smaller houses have also survived from this period. They include the pair of shops, nos. 38 and 40, north of the Spotted Dog in South Street and, a little further south, the house next to Vincent Walk, nos. 80 and 82. At 16 West Street there is a weather-boarded building with bays, and 32 and 33 are also early 18th century. Off Station Road, 9 Spring Gardens dates from c.1750. In the High Street, at the east end past the Post Office, there are nos. 179–193; in Dene Street by the entrance to Dene Street Gardens are nos. 37 and 38; and at the end of Dene Street, Cotmandene Lodge.

It is sad that one old cottage no longer exists, because it housed the Dorking eccentric, Major Peter Labelliere (1726–1800). Born in England of French parents, he served in the 92nd Regiment of Foot, and lived in a cottage known as 'The Hole in the Wall' behind Holder House in South Street. A cultivated man, he became negligent of his appearance, until known in the town as 'The Walking Dunghill'. He left explicit instructions about the manner of his funeral and burial, including a requirement for his landlady's two youngest children to dance on his coffin. He was buried upside down on Box Hill, where every visitor can now read his name. Claiming that the world was topsy-turvy, he wished to be right at the last.

Starvation and Riot

In the south of England generally, labourers and cottagers were seldom far from being paupers, and all were often classified together for administrative purposes, a responsibility of the parish, which arranged for indoor relief in its workhouse, and outdoor relief by supplementation of wages.

The cost of relief rose steadily: a poor rate of 1s. in the pound in 1670 rose to 3s. in 1787, and 8s. in 1817, levels which were deemed insupportable. This might have been avoided if wage rates had risen in line with inflation, particularly during the very inflationary period of the Napoleonic wars. But, although corn prices were high and profits were good, magistrates refused to set a minimum wage. At a time when introduction of farm machinery, such as threshing and reaping machines, was threatening further unemployment, it was easy for employers to resist wage demands.

In the winter of 1830, after a disastrous harvest, starving labourers rioted in the southern counties. Near Guildford a market was attacked, and farm machinery destroyed. Bands of men took to the hills; a sheep stolen from Dorking was traced to Holmbury Hill. At Trout's farm, south of Dorking, cornstacks were burnt. At Albury, to the west, a miller who was also an overseer of the poor, was called to his window at night by a mob, and a shot was fired, fortunately for him at the wrong window.

A mob meeting was arranged to be held outside the Wotton Hatch. When news of this reached Dorking, 53 special constables were assembled; they marched to Wotton, where the gathering was dispersed, but not before settling to meet again in Dorking itself on Monday 22 November. In alarm, the Dorking magistrates asked for a troop of cavalry to be quartered in the town: 50 sabres were mustered, but half of these were then sent on to Guildford. The Home Office sent a consignment of peace-officers' staves, painted black with the letters WR IV (William IV) in yellow. Any other available weapons were taken into the Red Lion for safe keeping, except for some pikes which had been stored in the church since the Napoleonic invasion scare; the staves of these were burnt, and the heads buried in the churchyard.

One hundred and fourteen special constables were sworn in from volunteer townsmen. On the appointed day, hundreds of labourers stormed through the neighbourhood, forcing young men from the villages to join them. The mob assembled outside the Red Lion, where the

Notice.

It has been made to appear to the Magistrates acting for the Hundred of Wotton, that Hand-bills have been circulated and stuck up in three of the Parishes of this Hundred, tending to excite discontent in the minds of the labouring Classes, and to create dissatisfaction and ill-will towards the Government, through the means of deception and misrepresentation, the Magistrates,—with a view to protect the honest labourer from the mischievous designs of men, known in this case to be strangers to the County, and to have no common interest with those whom they would mislead,—feel themselves called upon, in their characters of conservators of the public peace, and as the true friends of the labourers amongst whom they live, to warn them against the objects of these strangers, who, if they should excite them into violations of the law, would, as has been done on so many recent occasions, leave them to suffer the consequences of crime, which, but for such influence, they might never have thought of committing.

This caution,—given in the spirit of kindness and good-will, and in the most anxious desire to prevent the spread of those evils, which have so lately afflicted the adjacent Counties,—is called forth in consequence of its having come to the knowledge of the Magistrates, that an Agent, employed for that purpose by an Inhabitant Shopkeeper of HORSHAM, was sent on *Wednesday the 22nd. instant*, to distribute and post up Hand-bills of the character herein described, at the Public Houses and other places in the Parishes of CAPEL, OCKLEY and DORKING; and as the Magistrates have reason to believe, that the circulation of these mischievous publications is systematically pursued, they cannot too earnestly beseech the Inhabitants of this Hundred, carefully to guard themselves against these and any other attempts of designing Men, to render them the dupes of misrepresentations, which can have no honest purpose or intention.

BY ORDER OF THE MAGISTRATES,

THOMAS HART,

CLERK.

Dorking, Dec. 28th, 1830.

LANGLEY, PRINTER, DORKING.

Magistrates sat in the long room used as a courtroom. One of them, James Broadwood J.P., of Lyne House, Capel, was sent out to reason with the rioters. Speaking from the top of the steps which formed the main entrance to the inn, he appeared to be making headway, when there was an unfortunate occurrence; a riderless horse and cart packed with broomsticks came charging into the crowd.

It is hard to believe that this was accidental. Broomsticks were seized by the rioters, who attacked the hotel, smashing the windows and hurling in chunks of chalk and flint. The magistrates retreated into the hotel, bolting the door and leaving the force of constables outside to defend it. There followed a heavy and bloody fight, which was resolved by the arrival of the cavalry, who charged through the crowd, trampling and wounding. The battle was over. While magistrates reappeared to read the Riot Act, the constables dashed into the shattered crowd and arrested the ringleaders. The remainder were chased out of town by the cavalry.

The arrested men were taken to Guildford gaol. A crowd collected at Woking aiming to rescue them, but eventually dispersed. The ringleaders were transported, and others received heavy sentences of imprisonment.

The farmers paid their labourers an extra shilling a week for a little while, but stopped as soon as they felt safe again.

The use of troops to control civil disturbance was not at all unusual; governments were at all times nervous of revolution spreading from the Continent. In 1780 troops had been encamped on Ranmore because of the threat of riots in London. Their presence is recorded in the register of Dorking Congregational Church in the form of baptisms of children of soldiers from the Scots Greys, the Old Buffs, the 69th Regiment of Foot, and the Northumberland Militia.

Provision for the Poor

A workhouse for paupers seems to have been provided by use of Richard Browne's old almshouses of 1613 in South Street. Perhaps it was these buildings which a local Justice of the Peace, the Hon. Hugh Hare of Betchworth, had in mind when in 1692 (in a notable Charge to the Grand Jury delivered at Dorking) he recommended that fines for certain crimes, such as bloodshed, adultery, or swearing, should go to the poorhouse. By the early 18th century these old buildings were becoming inadequate to meet the needs of the poor either as almshouse or workhouse and, in 1728, a new poor house was built on an adjacent South Street site. On June 21 and 22 that year two men were employed to move the paupers from the old to the new house next door. The new house, costing £900, held 50–60 inmates. It was extended in 1795 for £270 and it was probably at this time that a new wing was added.

Overseers for the workhouse were appointed by annual contract. Under this system the overseer was free to make what profit he could out of the operation of the workhouse and abuses were inevitable, although as the 18th century progressed contracts became tighter and more detailed with regard to the overseer's responsibilities.

Old workhouse, South Street. *Watercolour by J. Hassell dated 1822. (Surrey Archaeological Society).*

The inmates were kept busy; in 1793 the overseer undertook in his contract to return to the inmates some small proportion of any profit caused by their labours. Records show how they worked in a woollen manufactory, were employed to watch the town, dug in the Barclay estate, or laboured at the Giles Green gravel pit. At the workhouse they brewed their own beer, worked in the workhouse field or operated the hand-flour mill; the latter, a particularly heavy job, was probably allocated as a punishment.

In 1819 a new Act permitted parishes to set up committees to scrutinise the granting of poor relief and from November 1820 to March 1821 the average weekly cost per head was reduced from 3s.5d to 1s. 10d. Then under the new Poor Law Amendment Act of 1834, Poor Law Commissioners took over general responsibility, creating the Union System, and providing for locally-elected Boards of Guardians.

The Dorking Union was created in 1836 to include the parishes of Abinger, Capel, Dorking*, Effingham, Mickleham, Newdigate, Ockley and Wotton. Its first task was to provide facilities for the numerous poor of the area. The old building was surveyed for its adequacy to meet new requirements, and found to be much decayed. The south-west wing was in better repair, and it is this part which survives as 1 and 2 South Street

---

* Dorking 'urban and rural parish', which included Holmwood, Westcott and Coldharbour.

Cottages, behind the buildings now forming the road frontage. The cost of repairs was too high and capacity of the house too low to satisfy the Commissioners, and in 1838 the decision was taken to build a new Union Workhouse.

This was erected on four acres of land further south, east of the Horsham Road; completed in 1841, it still stands, forming part of the Dorking General Hospital. Designed by William Shearburn Sr, to hold 250 paupers, it was laid out in the form of a square. In the centre were the kitchen and Master's quarters, with four arms radiating out to the perimeter, creating four easily supervisable yards. One of the first purchases was a bone-mill, deliberately chosen to be operated by a crank; with the easier capstan-type of operation, experience had shown that the men could ride round on the capstan arms.

The old building in South Street was largely demolished in 1845, but not without legal battles over ownership of the land which Richard Browne had originally donated for charitable purposes. The money raised from the sale of demolition materials helped to renovate the Cotmandene almshouses.

These newer almshouses had been built in 1677 when, perhaps because Richard Browne's almshouses in South Street were already becoming inadequate, Sir Adam Browne and the Hon. Charles Howard, joint lords of the manor of Dorking, gave on a 2000 year lease a portion of the manorial 'waste called Cotmandene' for the erection of an almshouse to contain 18 persons. Rebuilt in 1848 with the aid of the money mentioned above, and modernised and extended in 1961, they remain as an attractive part of the Cotmandene scene.

The almshouses received their first endowment in 1718, when a bequest of Mrs Susannah Smith, after a dispute in Chancery, was ordered to be applied for the maintenance of 'the poor old men and women in the hospital at Cotman Dean'. In 1831 Richard Lowndes of Rose Hill, purchased £300 in Reduced Consols and gave the interest of £3–12s. per annum to the almshouse in perpetuity. As a result of this addition each of the individual almspeople received an average of £1–18s. p.a. Dividends from other donations, such as £900 in 3% Consols, were also spent on their behalf.

The distinction between almshouse and workhouse has at times been fine or non-existent, but in principle the almspeople were maintained by charitable bequests, administered by local charity trustees, while before the new Poor Law of 1834 the workhouse was maintained by the parish. Parish officials also administered other charitable bequests made for the parish poor. Some bequests carried very precise instructions. In 1706 William Hutton left 6s. p.a. derived from a holding at Brockham, to be laid out on penny loaves to be distributed among the most needy poor in the church every Good Friday. In 1725 Mrs Margaret Fenwick left £800, which was used to buy an 80 acre farm called Fordland at Albury. The proceeds were to be applied to the apprenticing of poor children, and 'preferring in marriage such maid-servants as should have lived and behaved well for seven years in any one service'. Very few applications were received for the marriage portions; the surplus was distributed amongst the poor. In 1807 Thomas Summers left £100, the interest from which was to be spent by the churchwardens on bread for the poor every 1st January; and 40 poor widows shared £1 derived from the rent of 'Poor Folk's Close', a slip of land at the corner of Horsham and St. Paul's Roads.

The parish continued to administer the older charities, including that of Cosens mentioned in Chapter 4. Proceeds from Henry Smith's charity estate in Bottesford, Leicestershire, amounted in 1832 to £172–16s. p.a. Another of Smith's charities, invested in Longstock, Hampshire, gave an allotment to Dorking which, in 1844, amounted to £32–9s. All this income was spent on tickets for bread, meat or clothing given to the poor.

Religious Life

The ancient parish church of St. Martin's, described in a previous chapter, continued virtually unchanged throughout this period. By the late 17th century the church building was also in use as a school house, with reading, writing and Latin classes being held in different parts, and this continued into the early 19th century.

The vicarage for over 200 years had been a substantial house in Back Lane, now known as Church Street, at the south-western corner of its junction with North Street. The stable block still forms part of the cottages which lie back from North Street on the west side, while the arch built into the structure on the corner formed the entrance. These premises were abandoned in 1800, being said by then to be in a ruinous state. The vicar then moved to a handsome early 18th century house in South Street next to the Queen's Head, living there for over 30 years. This building was a victim of the motor age, demolished in 1930 to make room for road widening and May's Garage. In 1837–38 the Church Street property was sold, and a vicarage was then established in Sondes Place at the corner of Vincent Lane and Westcott Road. This served until 1986, when the Vicar moved to its modernised stable block, and the rest of this fine late 17th century house was converted to apartments.

In 1725 there was a visitation by the diocesan bishop, Bishop Willis of Winchester, in the records of which it was noted that there were about 300 Presbyterians and Quakers in the parish. Dorking was in fact a focus for Independents, who came from miles away for Sunday Services. Following the Declaration of Indulgence in 1672, licences to preach in Dorking had been issued to James Fisher and to John Wood, who founded the Independent Congregational Church in Dorking. A meeting house established in 1719 in West Street survived until 1834. The building which arose in its place (now the United Reformed Church), with its attractive Italianate frontage, was, like the new workhouse, designed by the Dorking architect and builder, William Shearburn Sr. It contained an organ which had originally been installed in the Royal Pavilion at Brighton. This rebuilding represented a great revival of fortunes for the church: following a steady fall in congregations in the 18th century, much of the revival in the 19th can be attributed to the Rev. Alfred Dawson, whose sermons had children clinging to the organ rails to make room for others.

On the west wall of this church there is a memorial tablet to Mary Alexander née Eives (1741–1833). She lost her parents, who were adherents of the Society of Independents, and was later cut out of her grandfather's will for refusing to marry in accord with his wishes. The man Alexander whom she married speculated fraudulently, and was eventually hanged at Tyburn. She came to live with a cousin in a house in West Street standing where the church gates are now sited, and became a leading figure in her church. One of the founders of the Sunday school in 1806, she was perhaps still influential when in 1816 the first public elementary school in Dorking, the non-denominational British School, was founded with a grant from the British and Foreign Schools Society, pre-dating the Anglican National School.

Methodism found a base in Dorking in the 18th century, although it had relatively little impact in the south east generally. John Wesley first visited Dorking on 12th January 1764, recording that his host did not want him to preach, so that in the evening he had nothing to do. But on the following Friday, 'in a broad place not far from the market place', he held forth, first to three children, but then to a gradually increasing audience, 'although the air was sharp. The audience behaved well, but for three or four gambling men, who stood so far off that they disturbed no-one but themselves'. This was the first of 19 visits over 22 years, and a society was established by 1770. Meetings were first held in a large room in a yard near the Red Lion, but a meeting house was established in 1772 in Back Lane (Church Street), and still stands beside the car park behind the King's Arms, having outlived its replacement, as described in the next chapter. Wesley paid his last visit to Dorking in 1789, recording that he 'laboured to arouse a harmless drowsy people who for many years have seemed to stand stark still, neither increasing nor decreasing'.

There were of course no Roman Catholic churches at this time, although Catholics were represented in the parish, not least by one of the most powerful families, the Howards, Lords of the Manor, who were duly noted at 'papists' by Bishop Willis. Even the 11th ('Protestant') Duke retained strong Roman Catholic sympathies.

Dorking at Leisure

Cotmandene, or the 'Heath', became famous for its cricket during the 18th century. Two-day games were held, attracting hundreds of spectators from the town and miles around. Dorking players were prominent in the Surrey County Cricket Club when this was formed in 1844.

Cricketer's-eye view of Dorking from Cotmandene, looking north west, 1821. Heath Hill in centre below the church, Ranmore in the background. *Engraving in Dorking Museum.*

Football was also played, but Dorking was better known for its Shrove Tuesday game, preceded by a grotesquely dressed band, and played by a large crowd through the streets of the town. The date when this custom started is not clear, some sources ascribing it to much earlier times, but it was certainly being observed in the early 19th century. Commencing at the church gates about 2 p.m., the ball would be kicked through the streets, and deliberately into the most objectionable places, such as the slaughter house offal heap in West Street, or into the wettest, such as the Pippbrook. The 'sport' was declared closed at 6 p.m. The last full game was played in the presence of 2,000 people in 1897. This riotous process, which caused shopkeepers to close and shutter their premises, and obstructed traffic, was clearly getting out of proportion for such a small town, and was suppressed from 1902. It had completely died out by 1910.

Theatrical companies visiting Dorking would play in the yards or rooms of some of the inns. The King's Head provided entertainment rooms, while in 1820 a sumptuous new ballroom was built at the Red Lion. In 1807, Collins, the artist, was writing to his friend, Mr. Moore, who lived near London Road, and described a visit to the 'theatre, Dorking', which 'most elegantly gratified the senses, that of smelling not excepted, there being four candles to light us all, two of which by nine o'clock (no doubt frightened by the company) hid themselves in their sockets'.

Because it was a market town Dorking contained many inns and public houses, which offered their traditional opportunities for relaxation. They were to be augmented in the 19th century by the beer houses, many of which, despite a number of losses in the 1960s and 1970s, survive as public houses. The house which offered the entertainment of fighting cocks in its cockpit cellars, The Wheatsheaf, had a proprietor, Mr. Philps, who was famous for raising large hogs. In 1750 he reared one said to be the largest ever seen in England, weighing 1,036 lbs. (471kg), young and still growing. Unfortunately while being exhibited, it vanished with its minder in the west of England. In 1767 Mr. Philps had a larger hog, but it broke a leg and was killed; stuffed and mounted, it became a showpiece of the house, 12ft. long, with 8ft. girth, and 13 hands high (4ft 4ins). Had it lived to be fatted, it could have tipped the scales at 2,800lbs (1,272kg).

By the early 19th century there were many opportunities and encouragements for reading, including a branch of the Bible Society and a circulating library, while a book society was established among the gentry of the town and neighbourhood. In 1820 a magazine society was started: for 15s. per annum the twenty founding subscribers received on circulation *The Monthly Magazine, Baldwin's Monthly Magazine, The Eclectic Review, The Imperial Magazine, Blackwood's Edinburgh Magazine, The Monthly Review,* and *The Journal of Modern Voyages and Travels;* the *Edinburgh Quarterly,* and *British Reviews;* and the annual *Times's Telescope* – a total of 100 numbers.

During the 18th century, Dorking gradually developed a reputation as a minor health and holiday resort; due, in the words of John Timbs, to the 'salubrity of the air, and the picturesque beauty of the scenery; a short residence here is frequently recommended to invalids by London practitioners, and is generally attended with speedy convalescence or essential benefit'.

The many visitors who thronged the town in summer could taste a local culinary delicacy known as water souchy, introduced originally by

Dutch merchants. It was prepared from the perch, carp and tench which teemed in the millponds and rivers, and was served at the local inns: the King's Head, and later the Red Lion, were both famous for it.

A London in Miniature

By 1830, with a literate and affluent society, and a population of 3,000, it was a transformed Dorking which faced the new Victorian age. The town, paved by public subscription in 1817–18, had seen the introduction of street lighting by oil lamps very soon afterwards. John Timbs in 1823 described it as 'a London in miniature, possessing shops little inferior in taste and display to the boasted lines of Cheapside and the Strand'.

He described a view from Ranmore of the town of Dorking, surrounded by handsome villas and genteel cottage residences; but he contrasted them with humble cottages in the same scene. Most of the latter, though

This view of c. 1829 includes the newly-built Dendy's Tower on the skyline and the chalkpits in the foreground. *Lithograph printed by C. Hullmandel. (Surrey Archaeological Society).*

sometimes picturesque, were insanitary and usually overcrowded and ill-ventilated hovels, barely fit for human habitation, and as we shall see, they were to attract the earnest attention of a more sophisticated local administration in the latter half of the 19th century. But at this point in time, with the new workhouse soon to be built on the southern hill, and a substantial proportion of its population on Poor Relief, Mr. Timbs' view from Ranmore symbolised a Dorking which was growing out of its depressed agricultural past, and was preparing itself for the new Victorian age.

Dorking from Meadowbank c. 1830, looking south east. *From Thomas Allen's 'History of Surrey'.*

The eastern entrance to Dorking, mid 19th century. Shrub Hill is seen left. *Engraving. (Dorking Museum)*

CHAPTER SIX

VICTORIAN PROGRESS AND GROWTH: 1837-1900

Alan A Jackson

Despite significant residential expansion, some increase in industrial activities and the opening of two railway lines, Dorking remained a self-supporting, somewhat sleepy country market town all through the 19th century. As such, it was held in great affection by its sons and daughters, and contemporaneous journalistic references to 'our dear old town' struck a genuine note.

Thanks largely to its market, Dorking served as a business and retail centre for surrounding rural communities up to six to eight miles away. From the 1830s this role was strengthened by administrative changes. As we have seen in Chapter 5, in 1836, under the Poor Law Amendment Act of two years earlier, the Dorking Union was formed, covering an area of some 40,520 acres around the town. The same group of parishes was established in 1874 as the Dorking Rural Sanitary District. And from 1845 onwards Dorking became the postal address and mail handling centre for most of this part of Surrey*.

New Industries Alongside the Old

Whilst the established industries of milling, brewing, malting, lime burning and the small iron foundry all continued to thrive, even expand in Victoria's reign, new ones also appeared. Although small scale brickmaking activities had long existed in the town, the period was notable for the establishment around 1870 of what eventually became the Dorking Brick Company's works, using the Wealden clay at North Holmwood to produce a high quality red brick of great hardness. New arrivals included a coal gas works (to be mentioned later); firestone quarrying, from about 1850 to about 1890, at a site between Chalkpit Lane and Ranmore Road; Taylor & Brooker's timber works and saw mills in Station Road, employing about 100 men by 1900; two candle manufactories on the west side of the town; and small factories producing mineral water, ginger beer and other soft drinks. These last were related to the seasonal visitors, who had become a major feature in the town's economy.

---

* By the end of the century Dorking Head Post Office controlled the sub offices at Abinger Common, Abinger Hammer, Beare Green, Capel, Coldharbour, Forest Green, Holmbury St Mary, Holmwood, Mickleham, Newdigate, Ockley, Ranmore Common, Westcott and West Humble.

Holidays, Tourists and Trippers

Short and long stay tourists and holidaymakers, attracted by the relaxing climate and fine scenery, had begun to patronise Dorking in the 18th century, but the convenience of the new railways, which reduced the journey from the metropolis to around an hour, compared with three to four by road, much stimulated the flow. On fine Sundays, and at Bank Holidays after the latter had been introduced in 1871, Box Hill and Cotmandene were favourite objectives for day excursions from London's suburbs and by the 1890s Easter, Whit or August Bank Holiday would see the arrival of 3,500 to 5,000 people by rail, with another 2,500 or so coming by road, many of them cyclists.

With the railway allowing father to travel daily to and from his work in the capital during part or most of the season, it became customary for middle class families to take a house in the town in summer. Invalids also came 'to enjoy the salubrity of the air and exhilarate their spirits by the loveliness of nature'*. One local paper regularly printed lists under

A popular view of the White Horse Hotel in c. 1870 taken from Louis J Jennings, *Field Paths & Green Lanes, 1877.* The near-contemporary G Phillips Bevan, *Tourists' Guide to the County of Surrey,* notes 'The highways to . . . Dorking . . . are also traversed during the summer months by well-horsed coaches, and this is a most enjoyable, though somewhat expensive, mode of traversing the prettiest districts more at leisure'.

the heading 'Dorking Visitors' during the summer season; in 1889 we find names of people staying at boarding houses and apartments in Rose Hill, West Street, Hampstead Road, South Street, High Street,

* Pigot's Directory, 1839

Horsham Road and Wathen Road. At this time it was also recorded that North Americans were fond of visiting the town, some patronising a horse coach driven down from London regularly in the season which brought them to the White Horse in time for a late luncheon.

Shops and Market

This visitor and holiday trade, combined with the buoyancy of the local industries, generated a gentle prosperity for the many shopkeepers of the High Street, West Street and South Street. With their horse-drawn delivery carts, they also built up further business by serving the surrounding villages, thus reinforcing the town's role as a focal point for its surrounding rural communities.

Dorking's tradespeople also profited from a new tendency for successful merchants, business and professional men and other wealthy members of the middle class to build themselves very large houses in the outskirts of the town, notably in the hill country to the south west. This colonisation of the Dorking hinterland by the prosperous, which continued until World War 1, can be related to the growth of the metropolitan upper middle class and to the convenient rail access to London. Such people could of course well afford their own horse-drawn transport to take them to and from the stations at Gomshall, Betchworth or Dorking.

Many of the names of the Victorian firms are still fondly remembered in the town, some surviving as business titles. People such as Charles J Rowe, stationer, printer and bookbinder of South Street (whose name is still in use at the premises opened by Charles' father in 1858); J & W Attlee, millers and corn merchants of High Street and Parsonage Mill, a family firm which traded in Dorking from 1788 until 1973; James Ivery & Son, nurserymen, seedsmen and florists, High Street and London Road; Herbert Croucher & Co., florists, fruiterers and greengrocers, South Street; Messrs Crow, land agents, auctioneers and valuers, South Street, who for many years, with White & Sons, High Street, were the motivators and organisers behind the market; A Chalcraft, seedsman & florist, South Street; Joseph Mason, grocer & provision merchant, High Street; Cummins & Sons, builders, Station Road; S W Fuller, cycle agent, established in South Street in 1892 and still controlled by the same family; Down, Scott & Down, solicitors, established in the High Street in 1855, and also surviving (as Downs); C J Pierson & Co, ironmongers & china merchants, High Street; T H Sherlock & Son, carriage builders and undertakers, West St, still in business in South Street; Robert Spratley, hairdresser, High Street; J Beetham-Wilson chemist and optician, High Street, dabbler in belladonna cultivation, radium experiments and purveyor of waterbeds; and Hart, Scales & Hodges, High Street, another firm of solicitors still in business, founded by John Hart, who died in harness at 87 in 1889 after practising in the town for 59 years.

As the retail trade prospered, many of the older premises in the High Street were refaced and refronted with results not always a visual improvement. High Street Buildings, dating from the 1880s and 1890s, terraces of shops with domestic accommodation above, some of them prettily decorated with terracotta, extended the retail centre eastwards beyond the Surrey Yeoman, a development which included the 1894 Oddfellows' Hall with shops below, designed by the local architect William Shearburn, Jr.

Dorking High Street on Market Day, looking east from Pump Corner, c. 1871. *Photograph, J. Chaplin. (N. E. C. Molyneux).*

One of the most popular buildings in the High Street was the Red Lion Family & Commercial Hotel, in the market place on the south side. This had some claim to be the principal hostelry in the town, its spacious accommodation finding many varied uses, and acting as a centre for judicial, administrative and commercial business and social activities. Its 1820 assembly room, destroyed in a disastrous fire in 1886, partly owing to the inefficiency of the Water Company, was handsomely renewed by the following year. That occasion was celebrated by a supper and ball at which sixty guests danced to 'the strains of a capital quadrille band until an early hour', to quote a local paper. Election results were announced from the steps up to the main door of the hotel, whilst at various times until the 1860s its rooms were used for monthly magistrates' courts. Licensing sessions, meetings of the Turnpike Trust, auction sales, sundry concerts, annual dinners of local organisations, even dental operations all took place within its walls. Licences for stage performances in the assembly rooms were granted by the Local Board from 1890.

Although the South Street poultry market had faded away by the 1870s, the main Thursday High Street livestock and corn market was tenuously sustained (with some breaks) throughout the Victorian period. In 1876 Jennings found the cattle market had been abandoned, noting that the corn market, 'if such it can be called' is chiefly carried on at the "Three Tuns"'. From 1886 the High Street market was limited to every fourth Thursday. Attempts at revival by the auctioneers Crow and White achieved limited success, and from the the 1890s the frequency was increased to fortnightly, with livestock again evident. During World War 1, weekly markets were again held and from March 1918, market day was changed to Monday. The manorial rights to market tolls and the market spaces in the town* were sold by the Duke of Norfolk to the Local Board of Health in 1891.

As mentioned in Chapter 5, an associated institution was the annual horse and fatstock fair, held on the day before Ascension day. Known also as the Dorking May Fair, this was still supplemented on that day, and on Ascension day, by a pleasure fair, originally located at Butter Hill/South Street but later moved to the Cotmandene. This fair continues today, though not always on the ancient dates. From around 1870 there also came into being a congested and lively Saturday night stallholders' and cheapjacks' market in the High Street, the various shouts and cries arising from it causing much distress to the adjacent residents and to the hotel managers, who alleged that this 'reproduction of Whitechapel in Dorking' cost them valued respectable custom. It was however to prove a resilient survivor, enjoying the protection of some councillors, who saw it as playing an important part in improving the life of the poorer people in the town.

The Coming of the Railways

Railway facilities arrived in 1849 with the opening of the Reading, Guildford & Reigate Railway Company's line from Redhill Junction to Guildford. The station, which included a goods yard, was sited somewhat remotely at the north western fringe of the town outside the then built-up area. Although still open today (as Dorking West) it is now a mere halt, denuded of its former importance. A second station (now Dorking Deepdene) was opened on the main London Road early in 1851. The new form of transport initially made little impact on the life of the town,

---

* Butter Hill, High Street and Spital Heath were named as sites, but no evidence has yet been found for use of the latter for market purposes.

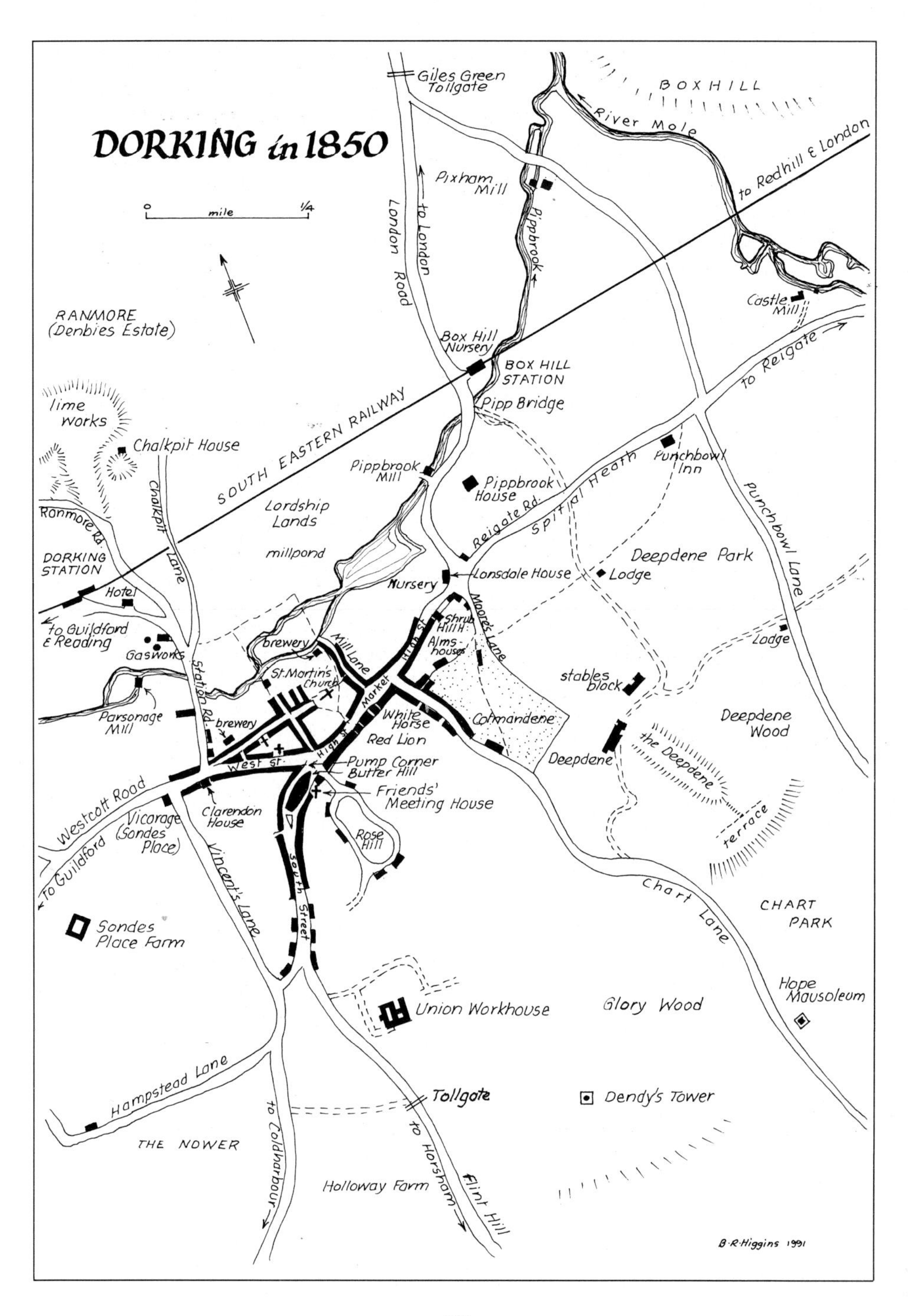
DORKING in 1850
0 mile 1/4
Giles Green Tollgate
BOXHILL
River Mole
to Redhill & London
Pixham Mill
Pippbrook
to London
London Road
RANMORE (Denbies Estate)
Castle Mill
to Reigate
Box Hill Nursery
BOX HILL STATION
SOUTH EASTERN RAILWAY
Pipp Bridge
lime works
Chalkpit House
Pippbrook Mill
Pippbrook House
Punchbowl Inn
Spitial Heath
Punchbowl Lane
Ranmore Rd.
Chalkpit Lane
Lordship Lands
Reigate Rd.
DORKING STATION
millpond
Deepdene Park
Hotel
Nursery
Lonsdale House
Lodge
to Guildford & Reading
Gasworks
brewery
Mill Lane
High St.
Shrub Hill
Moores Lane
Alms-houses
Lodge
Station Rd.
St. Martin's Church
Market
stables block
Parsonage Mill
brewery
White Horse
Red Lion
Cotmandene
Deepdene Wood
West St.
High St.
Pump Corner
Butter Hill
Deepdene
the Deepdene
Westcott Road
Friends' Meeting House
Clarendon House
Vicarage (Sondes Place)
Rose Hill
terrace
to Guildford
Vincent's Lane
South Street
Chart Lane
CHART PARK
Sondes Place Farm
Union Workhouse
Glory Wood
Hope Mausoleum
Hampstead Lane
Tollgate
Dendy's Tower
THE NOWER
to Coldharbour
to Horsham
Holloway Farm
Flint Hill
B.R.Higgins 1991

but things began to change when a second railway, providing a more direct route north eastwards to London and running southwards to Horsham, came into use in 1867. This was opened by the London Brighton & South Coast Railway Company, and its station, a pleasant two-storey building designed by Charles H Driver and built by Dorking's W J Shearburn, was sited a little to the north of the Deepdene platforms. There were facilities here for handling most types of traffic, also a small engine shed. With its rather more direct access to London, it eventually became the most important of the town's three stations for passenger business.

The South Eastern Railway station (now Dorking West) c. 1862, with Denbies in the background. *(Surrey Archaeological Society).*

An expanding population

Census figures* reflect the stimulus provided by the railways and the steady if unspectacular increase in prosperity. Broadly comparable figures for the urban parish are 3,058 in 1801, and 5,419 in 1871. After 1881, the figures relate to the same area and show growth from 6,328 inhabitants in 1881 to 7,132 in 1891 and 7,670 in 1901. The number of inhabited houses in the town rose from 612 in 1851 to 995 in 1871 and 1,425 in 1891.

Villas and Cottages

With the east-west railway and the Denbies lands forming a barrier to the north and the great Deepdene estate blocking the area to the

---

* See Appendix for more detail.

east and south east of the town, most of the new housing of the Victorian period was concentrated south and south-west of the ancient centre. This new provision was largely for the middle and artisan classes, the working class and the very poor, with one exception, continuing to occupy the picturesque if insanitary 18th and early 19th century cottages in the courts, alleys and narrow lanes off the central streets.

Perhaps the most attractive Victorian residential development was Rose Hill, a collection of Italianate and Tudor style villas built between 1838 and 1860 in the grounds of Rose Hill House, nicely arranged around a large steep-sloping paddock. It retains much of its charm today. Those houses at the top of the hill, facing north, were erected speculatively by the Dorking Villa Building Company, a local concern which existed for a century from 1846.

Between 1852 and 1870 Arundel and Howard Roads were filled with pleasantly-proportioned artisan houses. Further south, on curving and steep roads newly made around Arthur Dendy's 1829 tower (Tower

Dorking New Workhouse c. 1869, looking east, with newly-erected villas in Horsham Road in foreground. *Photograph (David Knight).*

Hill, South Terrace, Tower Hill Road and Harrow Road East), large middle class villas on extensive plots appeared very slowly between 1854 and 1870. Both these estates were developed by the National Freehold Land Society, as was the area embraced by Harrow Road West, Falkland Road, Hampstead Road, Horsham Road and Coldharbour Lane, a mixed grouping of middle class and artisan villas, tenement and cottage housing mostly dating from 1856–75. The meaner property erected in Falkland Road, Falkland Hill, Falkland Gardens and Hampstead Road was almost unique for new construction in the town at this date. It soon deteriorated. Much of this 'Falkland District' attracted the attention of the Medical Officer of Health in the 1920s and almost all was condemned for demolition as sub-standard in 1959–70.

The 1880s saw the development of the middle class Cliftonville (named after its creator, Joseph Clift, High Street chemist and member of the Local Board), and also some villas in nearby Horsham Road and St Paul's Road West. Holloway Farm Estate was sold for villa development in 1870 and after the construction of Knoll, Roman and Ridgeway Roads, received its first houses around 1880. Building here, as at Tower Hill was slow to take off. Many of these houses were large, with attic storeys for servants, and cellars. In 1914 Knoll Road was described as 'one of the best residential roads in Dorking', for which the residents demanded gravel paths instead of the tarred footways normally provided by the Council. Also appearing in the 1880s were the tall south-facing blocks at the northern corner of Cotmandene, with their suggestion of seaside architecture, and in fact designed to be let to holiday makers as furnished apartments.

During the last two decades of the 19th century, artisan and lower middle class semi–detached and terrace houses were going up on the Wathen or Shrub Hill Estate, (Rothes Road, Ansell Road, Wathen Road, Hart Road, and Jubilee Terrace). Over a hundred houses had been built here by the middle of 1891. Contemporary with this development were the houses and cottages in Lincoln Road and the London Road villas between there and Deepdene station. Finally, from 1897, Lonsdale Road and the eastern part of Rothes Road were laid out on the Dorking Nurseries site.

During the 1890s this almost continuous house- building activity seemed about to slow almost to a stop, since the demand had for the time being been met. It was a situation which gave concern to the new (1892) Town Improvement Association, whose chairman speculated as to how all the shops could be successfuly maintained 'without an increase in the number of villa residents'.

Mansions for the Wealthy

Although modern commercial pressures have caused much destruction of the Victorian residential provision (particularly on Tower Hill) two fine mansions by noted architects of the period still survive.

The Gothic Renaissance Pippbrook, choicely sited against the backdrop of Ranmore and Box Hill, was built in stone in 1856 for the wealthy master of the Glamorgan Ironworks, William Henry Forman. It replaced a plain stuccoed house on the same site, latterly occupied by William Crawford, MP for the City of London, followed by his son.

Although designed in the office of Sir George Gilbert Scott, Pippbrook's somewhat uninspired elevations suggest that this great and busy practitioner took little personal interest in the project. However, the richly-decorated interior, much of which survives, is very fine*.

Goodwyns Place, designed by H. Thackeray Turner, was erected for the wealthy T. E. Powell, who died before it was completed in 1901. From 1918 until 1953 this elegant house, impressively-sited at the crest of Tower Hill on a south-facing escarpment, was the home of another Dorking benefactor, Howard Martineau, of the famous sugar and syrup firm. Sold in 1954, Goodwyns was first converted into laboratories and offices, then in 1987 handsomely refurbished to provide residential apartments.

A Glut of Churches and Chapels

Residential growth brought with it the usual lavish Victorian provision for Christian worship. The inadequate and decaying parish church had been largely rebuilt to the designs of William McIntosh Brookes to

The 'Intermediate' Parish church, c. 1871, looking south from Meadowbank. Deepdene Hills at left. *Photograph J. Chaplin. (N. E. C. Molyneux).*

---

* Sadly, two fine stone Scott fireplaces were hastily removed in 1973 to accommodate an expanded council, which soon enough would require a new building.

become the so-called Intermediate Church, completed in 1837. But this did not satisfy, and in turn gave way to the present building, one of Henry Woodyer's finest works, in the Decorated style, and magnificently proportioned. Building started in 1868 and was finally completed in 1877. With its 210ft spire (a memorial to Bishop Samuel Wilberforce), its high roof line and its central location, the church dominates its secular surroundings like no other in Surrey.

Woodyer's Parish Church of 1877 from a similar viewpoint to the picture on page 76, 1905. *Postcard. (John Coombes).*

To accommodate the Anglican demand from the growing southern suburbs, St. Paul's Church was completed in 1857 to the designs of Benjamin Ferrey, who also provided a pleasing vicarage. Looking down upon these two churches, 700ft up on Ranmore, close to Denbies, is Sir George Gilbert Scott's beautiful little St. Barnabas, erected in 1859 in Gothic Revival style as an estate church for Thomas Cubitt's son, George (later the first Lord Ashcombe). This community, then numbering some 400, was also provided with a school and rectory to match, all from drawings made in Scott's office. The central 150ft tower of the church supports a spire which rises above the trees on the Ranmore summit, earning the nickname 'Cubitt's Finger' from the poet George Meredith, who often walked here from his home at Flint Cottage, Box Hill. At Pixham, an eastern suburb of Dorking, an 'iron room' erected in 1883 was dedicated seven years later to cater for the spiritual needs of an isolated community at the eastern edge of the town, which had somewhat expanded after the opening of the two railway stations nearby. The site was transformed in 1903, when the hut gave place to an elegant dual-purpose church/clubroom, designed by the great architect Edwin Lutyens.

Roman Catholics were at first served by a small chapel and school erected off Coldharbour Lane in 1871–2. These were followed by St. Joseph's Church, built in Falkland Grove in 1895 to the designs of Frederick Arthur Walters on a site donated by the Duke of Norfolk, who also made a substantial contribution to the cost.

As we have seen, non-conformism has always been a strong force in the town. Congregationalists (now the United Reformed Church) worshipped in the West Street church mentioned in the previous chapter; Sunday Schools were erected behind it in 1859 and greatly enlarged, with the church, in the 1900s. Wesleyan Methodists held services at Ebenezer Row on the north side of East (High) Street from 1842–51, moving to a small church in Back Lane (Church Street) until 1900. They then built a fine new church and hall in South Street, at the corner of Vincent Road. Designed in Gothic Revival style, with a 90ft spire, this edifice was completed in 1901. It lasted only until 1974, the proceeds from the sale of its site going towards the construction of the 1977 Christian Centre alongside the parish church, which the Methodists had been sharing with the Anglicans since 1973. Baptists have worshipped in the town since 1869. Their chapel in Junction Road, completed in 1876, was considerably altered in 1902 to provide accommodation for 400. The Strict Baptists erected their own chapel behind High Street Buildings in 1910.

Quakers, active in Dorking since the beginning of the 18th century, established their first Meeting House behind West Street in 1709, moving in 1846 to the pleasingly elegant, if suitably plain, building on Butter Hill, made large enough to meet the needs of Friends from a large area around the town. A flint-faced Gospel Hall was erected in Hampstead Road in 1863 by the Open Brethren. Dorking's contingent of Exclusive Brethren followed the Methodists into Ebenezer Row, moving to a new building in Hart Road at the Council's expense in the 1980s when the site was required for a car park. Considerable controversy was aroused by the street musical activities of the Salvation Army after their 1887 arrival in a town so devoted to peace and quiet. Pressed into action by the Local Board, the forces of law and order caused the intrepid disturbers of Sabbath hush to spend a brief sojourn in Wandsworth Prison. On their return to Dorking, they were greeted at the railway station by their Brothers and Sisters and escorted like returning heroes in procession to the town.

Amidst all this enthusiasm, even the homeless poor were not left without premises for worship. In 1890 'a pretty little chapel' was dedicated at the Workhouse by the Bishop of Guildford.

More Room for the Dead

Nor were the dead neglected. With the churchyard approaching saturation, a beautifully-sited four-acre cemetery was opened in 1855 in the Reigate Road, offering mourners superb vistas of Box Hill and the Mickleham Gap. Entry was gained via a Gothic ornamental gateway and this together with Anglican and Nonconformist chapels, all to the designs of H. Clutton, was completed a year later. By 1889 there had been 3,456 burials here and an eastern extension of over five acres was acquired. Another three acres were added in 1923.

Glorious Deepdene

During the Victorian era, the great house and estate of Deepdene was at the apex of its splendour. Amongst famous visitors was Benjamin Disraeli, who recorded that his novel *Coningsby* was 'conceived and partly executed amid the glades and galleries of Deepdene'. In his *Tourists' Guide to the County of Surrey* (1887), G. Phillips Bevan wrote: 'The great sight of Dorking is Deepdene . . . one of the loveliest places in England, with a splendid art collection and charming grounds . . . The Dene (from which the house is named), is an exquisite glade at the back, in which landscape gardening is carried to the highest pitch, the trees being of specially rare and varied character.' To this arcadia in February 1894 came Lily, Duchess of Marlborough (1855–1909). Married in the following year to Col. Lord William Beresford VC, Lily, daughter of a US Naval Commodore, had obtained her title on her second marriage, to the Duke of Marlborough. She was thus an aunt of Winston Churchill, who often stayed with her at Deepdene. After her third husband died in 1900, the Duchess spent the last nine years of her life in the mansion. Much loved by the people of Dorking, she is commemorated by an attractive opus sectile art nouveau memorial in St. Martin's Church.

The Cubitts at Denbies

Immediately north west of the town lay another great estate, the 3,900 acres of Denbies, purchased in 1850 from Lord Londesborough, grandson of William Denison, by the successful London builder, Thomas Cubitt. Seeking to rival Deepdene across the vale, Cubitt constructed a grandiose new mansion with almost 100 rooms to replace the 18th century house erected by Johnathan Tyers. This huge brick and stucco structure, with its Italianate detail, followed the style of Cubitt's town houses and the east wing of Osborne, Isle of Wight, which he had built for Queen Victoria. Prince Albert was persuaded to inspect the new estate on 15 July 1851. But all was barely finished when Cubitt died amidst his earthly glory on 20 December 1855. His son George (1828–1917), who inherited, was a true 'improving landowner', developing the estate, which eventually gave employment to some 400. An MP from 1860, and made a Privy Counsellor twenty years later. George became the first 'Baron Ashcombe of Dorking and Bodiam Castle' in 1892. This title was derived from Ashcombe Hill, an old name for part of the estate area.

Gas, Water and a Hospital

As elsewhere, the Victorian period saw progressive expansion of public utilities and services. The Dorking Gas Light Company, founded as early as 1834, was very much a local enterprise, all its shareholders but one residing in the the town. A works was established in what later became Station Road and within a short time the main streets were gaslit. Further land was acquired for expansion of the works in 1882, 1896 and in 1902, when the number of consumers exceeded 500. The undertaking was reconstituted as the Dorking Gas Company in 1871. By 1894 there were 200 public lamps, two with triple burners, the rest ordinary jets, all provided and maintained by the company. Its employees lit and extinguished them, using a long pole, usually managing to do this whilst continuing to ride a bicycle. Around the turn of the century, the somewhat dim jets of the street lamps were converted to the much brighter incandescent mantle system.

Cottage Hospital, South Terrace, c. 1905, looking north-west. *Postcard (Alan A. Jackson).*

A Dorking Water Company established in 1869, with boreholes, pumping station and reservoir at Tower Hill, was also a very local concern. Initially this private enterprise faced much criticism over both the quantity and quality of its supply, so much so that by the end of the 1890s even Dorking's predominantly Conservative council was moved to threaten it with municipalisation. Thus goaded into action, the company arranged new sources; gravitation of soft water from springs in Redlands Wood (west of Mid-Holmwood) and a borehole and pumping station on the Deepdene Estate. Despite these additions, the situation still remained unsatisfactory at the opening of the new century.

The mid-Victorian Cottage Hospital Movement, originating in Surrey, achieved early success in Dorking. An elevated site in South Terrace was granted at peppercorn rent by Mrs. A. A. Hope of Deepene and a building containing seven beds and three cots was completed in 1871. Supported by voluntary contributions, this homely looking structure was enlarged in 1896 and again in 1907, when it had a total of 17 beds and a small operating theatre.

Municipal Improvements

Important advances followed the appointment of a Local Board of Health to succeed the Vestry in 1881. This new body was charged with responsibility for maintaining the roads, footpaths and street lighting and for organising refuse collection and a sewerage scheme. Drains and refuse were very much a priority.

In the late 18th and early 19th century shallow brickwork pipes had been provided under the main roads by the Turnpike Trust and the Highways Board to drain off surface water into the Pippbrook. But by the 1860s many domestic water closets of varying efficiency had been illegally connected to these outlets, transforming the stream to a foul smelling open sewer and killing all its fish. Working conditions at the Pippbrook and Pixham water mills can be imagined. Other households deposited their human and domestic waste into badly built and sited cess pits, mostly through improperly-ventilated pipes without traps. Since there was no collection of domestic refuse from the growing number of houses, stinking piles of rubbish proliferated. As well as contributing to the spread of disease, this state of affairs imparted a pervasive and increasing stench in every part of the town. In December 1873 the editor of *The West Surrey Times* was moved to comment: 'Do not the unpleasant odours in our streets, too frequently assailing the resident inhabitants, and so ominously enquired about by visitors, demonstrate the existence of nuisance heaps, the defective trapping of drains or the imperfection of sewerage?'

Remedying this situation, a priority fully recognised by the wisest heads, was to prove a long and costly exercise. Although the first sewerage scheme was proposed in 1872 and a Dorking Rural Sanitary Authority was established two years later, it was not until after the formation of the Local Board in 1881 that any progress was made. Work started in 1885 and the new sewerage system, with its 11½ acre outfall works at Pixham came into partial use in mid-1888. It was another four years before something like 95 per cent coverage of the urban area was achieved, with 1,360 houses connected. Even then, there remained the problem of extending cistern flushing to many houses. Worse still, the Pixham Works were soon found to be badly designed and engineered, requiring a major reconstruction in 1893.

The new Local Board quickly introduced regular collection of domestic refuse, selling it to farmers to spread over their fields. This, with the often squalid housing of agricultural workers and the dust and mud from the unsurfaced roads no doubt produced a rural environment rather less idyllic than it may seem to us when looking at contemporary paintings and photographs. A refuse destructor, burning the combustible matter and sorting out the residue, was opened in Station Road in 1910.

In its first year the Local Board also set about naming and numbering the streets, courts and yards in the town. Roads were a constant anxiety. In these last decades before the arrival of the motor car, the principal streets lacked a hard sealed surface and were covered with gravel. After rain they were transformed into rutted mud, whilst in dry weather watering was necessary to keep down the dust. Stone or hardwood crossing places were provided at busy points to give some protection to pedestrians.

Improvements to the drainage of the town brought to light another social problem. In 1890 the chairman of the Local Board remarked that whilst going round with the sewerage committee, he had been taken aback at the state of many of the cottages; he had no idea such places existed in the town, they were 'something disgraceful and not fit for human beings to live in'. Central government legislation passed that year allowed the Board to inspect insanitary and overcrowded property and to force owners to make necessary improvements or, in extreme cases, require demolition. In 1891, to its great credit, the Local Board embarked on a systematic survey of this dark side of Dorking and in the first four years, 109 dwellings had been more or less improved, although many remained to be inspected. It was to prove a long haul; as we shall see, Dorking's slums were not to be finally expunged until the 1960s.

In January 1895 a Dorking Urban District Council (UDC) was elected to take over from the Local Board, covering the same area. Seven years later, the UDC moved into purpose built offices at the north corner of South Street and Junction Road, designed and erected by the local architect William Shearburn Jr and occupying a site purchased by the Duchess of Marlborough, who leased it at a favourable rent.

Post Offices

Until 1932 this South Street building (purchased by the UDC in 1924) also housed the main Post Office on its ground floor. In 1845 a Post Office had been opened at the corner of North Street and High Street at the front of the old King's Head Inn. There were then but two postmen delivering in the town and three for the rural rounds, which extended as far as Abinger, Capel, Mickleham and Ockley. Telegraph service started in 1870, and until the move to South Street in 1902, the telegraph boys were required to wait in the Kings Head Yard until midnight, prepared to deliver any telegrams which might come in.

A Public Hall, a Fire Brigade and a Swimming Bath

1871 saw the erection by a private company of a Public Hall at the western end of West Street. Sometimes misnamed the 'town hall', and built to the designs of Charles Driver and Charles H. Rew, this fearsomely ugly pile soon proved indispensable for all kinds of functions and meetings, as well as theatrical performances. It was also used for some years by the Boy's High School and for Petty Sessions and County Court hearings. Part of the ground floor was to become the headquarters of the Volunteer Fire Brigade, which had been formed in 1870. With a call-out strength of six officers and 17 men, and equipped with a manual escape and two steam pumps, the brigade moved here from South Street in 1881.

Another Victorian public amenity initiated by local private enterprise was the covered swimming bath, opened in Station Road in 1893. Despite considerable assistance from the master of Denbies, this venture was fraught with financial and other problems and was taken over by the UDC in 1900. Its foundations proved inadequate for its difficult site and the leaks which had shown up from the start continued throughout its existence.

Magistrates' Court, Police and Open Spaces

After many years of making do in unsuitable accommodation, the magistrates moved into a purpose-built court building at the east end of the High Street in 1894. These premises included a police station to replace the inadequate installation in South Street and a small villa for the police superintendent. Dorking Police Division remained here until 1938, when it was transferred to its present location in Moore's Road.

Until 1897 there were no public open spaces in the town but to celebrate the Queen's Diamond Jubilee, the Duke of Norfolk offered the manorial Cotmandene common to the UDC with the qualification that it was 'to remain as a perpetual ornament and pleasure to the town', a requirement surely contravened by today's uncontrolled car parking. Townspeople were also allowed generous access to the Nower by the Barclay family of Bury Hill, a privilege much prized.

Schools

Public education facilities advanced somewhat less impressively than other services. A Dorking Boy's High School, formed in January 1884, began its existence on the top floor of the Public Hall, moving in 1892 to the Chart Lane Institute, a building provided twenty years earlier by John Evelyn of Wotton Place as an amenity for working men, but which had proved something of a failure in that respect. One result of this relocation to more suitable premises was greater participation by the newly-formed Surrey County Council, bringing grants for technical instruction and endowments for scholarships which, at least in theory, opened up access to secondary education for boys from the poorer families in the town for the first time.

There was no similar provision for older girls until 1903, when the St. Martin's (Church of England) High School opened in a corrugated iron room in Junction Road. In 1908 more commodious premises were obtained at Parsonage House, Station Road, but for another quarter of a century, the school's capacity and finances remained totally inadequate for the needs of the expanding population in and around Dorking. Girls unable to obtain a place were obliged to cycle what were often long distances daily, in all weathers, to the SECR (later SR) station, whence they travelled by train to Redhill for their secondary education.

The 1816 non-denominational British School moved in 1898 from its insanitary and overcrowded building in what is now Church Street to a new home in Norfolk Road. This was made possible by the efforts and charity of Miss E. M. Corderoy and her wealthy friend T. E. Powell, and as a tribute to them, it was renamed the Powell-Corderoy School in 1906.

A National (Church of England) School was set up in 1818 in a building immediately north west of the churchyard, later moving to another behind the High Street. More suitable new premises in West Street were occupied in 1862. Enlarged in 1879 and 1890, this West Street building was to remain in use until 1985.

Two more Anglican schools followed: St. Paul's, east of that church, in 1860 (with an infants' department added at Falkland Road in 1868); and Pixham Infants' School in 1880. For Roman Catholics, St Joseph's School was inaugurated in 1873, and this survives, although the Priory Convent School of 1888 was closed in 1974.

Reflecting the town's strong middle class base, Victorian private schools were numerous, if ephemeral. They included Clarendon House Mathematical & Commercial School for Boys at the bottom of West Street, which closed in 1883, its pupils going to the new High School. Dudley House, South Street catered for 'young ladies', both boarding and day pupils, from about 1888, whilst at Ivy Holt, a large house in London Road demolished in 1929, there was a preparatory school for boys. In the last decades of the century, a Miss Napper operated a small kindergarten at 6 Jubilee Terrace. James Moore's grammar school for boys, at the corner of the eponymous road and High Street, became the John Box School in 1867 when it was taken over by Box, who had been principal of the British School for five years. Gerard Olivier (father of the actor, Sir Laurence) ran a preparatory school at Tower Hill until he was ordained in 1904.

By the end of the century or soon after, Dudley House, John Box and Ivy Holt had all faded away, but Ebor House (in St. Paul's Road, for 'the daughters of gentlefolk'), Burchet House School for Girls (in South Terrace), the Fairbank School for Girls (Rose Hill) and the Cunningham Preparatory School for boys and kindergarten (in South Street) quickly appeared in their place.

Evening classes, initially confined to 'science, domestic arts and horticulture' were started at the Chart Lane Institute in 1892, beginning a long tradition of adult education which still survives in this building.

Matters Military

Towards the end of the Victorian era, Dorking's situation at the south end of the Mole Gap began to exercise the military mind. A peculiar and eventually international notoriety was achieved when the town and its surroundings became the subject of an imaginative work of fiction, *The Battle of Dorking,* which first appeared anonymously in *Blackwood's Magazine* in 1871. The author, Sir George Chesney, portrayed a Continental power (Germany, thinly disguised) with designs for world domination, invading England at a moment when she was weakly protected and unprepared. A central feature of his book was a fierce battle at Dorking, an obvious strategic point between the south coast landing places of any invading army and London. The War Office was gradually moved to accept this scenario as a practical possibility and by 1889 a local paper was reporting that war games based on the area were taking place at the Horse Guards in London. Staff officers were also observed prowling about the heights of Ranmore and very soon sites were selected for a chain of infantry 'forts' (more accurately described as lightly fortified mobilisation centres and equipment stores) along the top of the North Downs, two of them overlooking Dorking. These structures were duly erected in 1896 at Ranmore and Box Hill, but were hardly completed when the land battle concept was replaced by a policy switch which placed renewed faith in the invincibility of a strengthened Royal Navy.

Dorking had its own company of Volunteers (later Territorials) and in 1889 the Hon. George Cubitt (later Lord Ashcombe) provided land and funds for a fine Drill Hall, west of Station Road. The 'forts' had been designed for such auxiliary forces and in those last two decades of the 19th century, many local men no doubt drilled and manoeuvred with a special enthusiasm, convinced they might one day fight a real Battle of

Dorking. Curiously Chesney's book came to life again in 1940 when a new edition of the Dorking-based story was issued to Hitler's Army under the title *Was England Erwartet* (What England Awaits).

Dorking At The End of the Victorian Era

As the century drew to a close, the editor of the local paper looked back over Victoria's long reign. Whilst noting such factors as residential development, the main drainage scheme and a movement of the town's trade away from an almost total dependence on agriculture, he concluded that Dorking had not greatly changed: 'Therein lies one of its greatest charms. For those who visit it, Dorking has an old world aspect that is very delightful . . . nor have the amenities of the town suffered at the hands of modern commercial enterprise in the way that the amenities of other towns have suffered'.

Although the next hundred years would see more rapid change, much of it associated with that decidedly mixed blessing, the motor vehicle (S. W. Fuller of South Street had bought the town's first car in 1899), it is pleasant to record that there is much in the Dorking of the 1990s which that editor would be able to recognise as familiar. And not only its buildings and scenery: he would be pleased to find that the affection for the town in the hearts of many of its inhabitants, which so patently existed in his time, lives on.

CHAPTER SEVEN

THE TOWN IN THE MOTOR AGE: 1901–1991

Alan A Jackson

Dorking's history over the last hundred years has been one of increasing subjection to the dominant and powerful influence of the adjacent metropolis and of environmental changes (usually deleterious) to meet the unrelenting demands of motorised road transport and, for many years, those of a fast-growing population.

Population growth was most marked in the first half of the century. Between 1901 and 1931, the inhabitants of the UDC area grew from 7,670 to 10,109. In 1933 the UDC boundaries were extended to include the adjoining village communities, and taking this into account, the figures are 13,207 in 1921, and 22,594 in 1961. But the 1971 count showed a decrease of 240 on the previous figure and although the boundaries changed again in 1974, the lack of sites for further building continued to inhibit more growth in the town and its immediate surroundings.*

Change for industries and market

In the early decades of the new century the importance of the traditional local manufacturing and processing activities faded away, to be replaced after World War 2 by service activities, notably insurance, travel, engineering design and computer-related businesses. The lime works below Ranmore closed at the beginning of World War 2, parts of the pits later becoming a controlled tip for domestic refuse, and the 50-acre brick works at North Holmwood, enlarged in 1960 and still at that time producing 15 million bricks a year, ceased production in 1981. Dorking Iron Foundry stopped operating as such in 1950, the firm moving from West Street to new premises in Curtis Road in 1972. By 1912 no beer was being brewed in the town and the three maltings were no longer in use. Attlee's Parsonage Mill, which ceased to employ water power about 1919, was demolished in 1959, seed and grain processing continuing in new buildings. Pixham watermill closed in 1910, Pippbrook in 1932, and Castle Mill twenty years later.

In 1932 there were still as many as 87 different vendors on the agricultural and poultry side of the weekly Monday market but its importance in these categories declined in the 1950s and the last regular livestock market was held in December 1965. A stallholders' market survives, still bringing people from the surrounding villages to give the town additional bustle on Fridays.

---

* For more details of population changes see Appendix.

Tourism and Trippers Fade Away

Although all but a trickle of residential tourist trade had gone by the mid 1920s, lower middle class and working class day trippers continued to arrive in substantial numbers on fine weekends until the 1950s, encouraged from 1914 by the new motor omnibus services, and from 1925 by the electrification of the direct rail routes from south London. Whit Monday 1947 saw what was probably the largest invasion of this kind; on that day 14,000 passengers were dealt with at Box Hill station and another 12,000 at Dorking North, in addition to crowds coming in by bicycle, bus and car. From the late 1950s, with car ownership growing remorselessly, London's leisure crowds dispersed themselves far more widely.

Shops and Services

Although losing some business to the London departmental stores after these had introduced motor van delivery services in the early 1910s, the locally-based retail trade continued to prosper in the first decades of the century. A 1934 directory reveals great variety, with 103 separate trades, professions and services, including a masseur, 8 dentists, 10 doctors, 10 hairdressers, 10 bakers, 11 outfitters, 11 builders, 12 drapers, 12 greengrocers and fruiterers, 14 boot and shoe shops, 14 tearooms and restaurants, 14 menswear shops and tailors, 15 butchers, 16 motor garages and service stations, 17 tobacconists, 23 confectioners, and 23 grocers. Licensed premises had fallen to 24 and would continue to shrink as the market activities declined. At this time there were 242 retail outlets, 114 in the High Street, 45 in South Street, 40 in West Street and 10 in Dene Street, with the rest scattered around the back streets. Competition from the multiples was growing: by the end of the 1930s, W. H. Smith, Boots, Woolworths, Macfisheries, Timothy White, Montague Burton, J. Sainsbury and Freeman Hardy & Willis were ensconced on prime High Street sites.

From around 1960, pressures on the small retailers intensified as shopping patterns changed and supermarkets appeared. H. G. Kingham & Co. were retail and wholesale grocers and wine & spirit merchants, established in the town in 1893, with their main premises at 20–28 High Street, 14 branches in Surrey, Sussex and Kent, and a wholesale warehouse in Station Road. But they found they could not compete with supermarkets, selling out to Cullen's in 1969. Cullen's then gave up Dorking after less than two years. Charles Degenhardt, drapers and outfitters of South Street, had in 1906 taken over a shop established in 1853 and subsequently enlarged their premises but were obliged to close down in 1979 when, the family managers having reached retirement age, no buyer could be found to take over the shop as a going concern. Stone & Turner, ironmongers and hardware merchants, sold out to Robert Dyas in 1966 after 90 years of local trading. The Attlee family

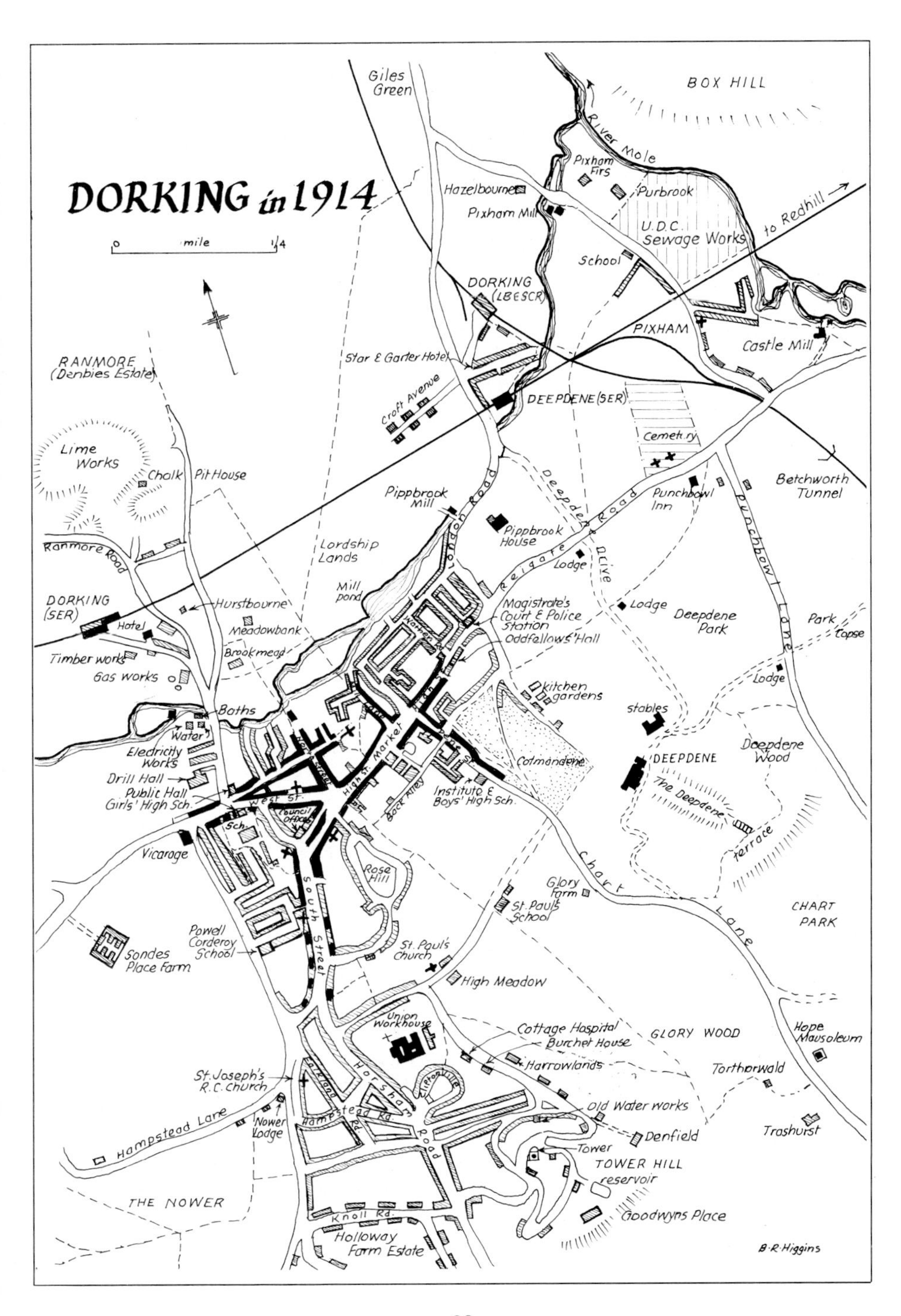
DORKING in 1914
0 mile 1/4
Giles Green
BOX HILL
River Mole
Pixham Firs
Purbrook
Hazelbourne
Pixham Mill
U.D.C. Sewage Works
to Redhill
School
DORKING (LBESCR)
PIXHAM
Castle Mill
RANMORE (Denbies Estate)
Star & Garter Hotel
Croft Avenue
DEEPDENE (SER)
Cemetery
Lime Works
Chalk Pit House
Betchworth Tunnel
Pippbrook Mill
Pippbrook House
Punchbowl Inn
Deepdene Drive
Reigate Road
Punchbowl Lane
Lordship Lands
Ranmore Road
Lodge
Mill pond
DORKING (SER)
Hurstbourne
Magistrate's Court & Police Station
Lodge
Deepdene Park
Park Copse
Hotel
Meadowbank
Oddfellows' Hall
Timber works
Brookmead
London Road
Gas works
kitchen gardens
Lodge
Baths
stables
Water
Electricity Works
High St.
Market
Cotmandene
DEEPDENE
Deepdene Wood
Drill Hall
Public Hall
Girls' High Sch.
West St.
Back Alley
Institute & Boys' High Sch.
The Deepdene
terrace
Sch.
Council Offices
Vicarage
Rose Hill
South Street
Chart Lane
Glory Farm
St. Paul's School
CHART PARK
Powell Corderoy School
Sondes Place Farm
St. Paul's Church
High Meadow
Union Workhouse
Cottage Hospital
Burchet House
GLORY WOOD
Hope Mausoleum
Harrowlands
Torthorwald
St. Joseph's R.C. Church
Horsham Road
Hampstead Rd.
Old Water works
Hampstead Lane
Nower Lodge
Denfield
Trashurst
Tower
TOWER HILL
reservoir
THE NOWER
Goodwyns Place
Knoll Rd.
Holloway Farm Estate
B.R.Higgins

of millers and corn and seed merchants, active in the town since 1788, sold the business out of the family in 1973. Unable to compete with the big names, the last of the mineral water and soft drink manufacturers established to succour the tripper trade closed down in 1967.

Even so, many independent small retailers showed a remarkable tenacity, a substantial core surviving into the 1990s to become one of Dorking's major assets, reinforced, from the 1960s onwards, by the development of a very active antiques centre, based along West Street. The last decade of the century saw submersion of the 1926 market area and its immediate environs under St. Martin's Walk, a new retail and office complex opened in 1991. With a Marks & Spencer foodstore as its anchor tenant, this neo-vernacular styled development (architects RHWL) included 26 other shops, 13,000 sq ft of offices, ten flats and 425 car spaces as well as accommodation for the Friday market. At the time of writing it is too early to assess its effect on the remainder of the town's retail businesses.

Residential Expansion

Economic conditions were highly favourable to residential building all around London in the 1920s and 1930s, a process aided in Dorking by the breakup of the Deepdene and Pippbrook estates, the 1921 sale of sections of the Denbies estate on the western edge of the town and, a few years later, the development of those parts of the Denbies lands close to the North and Deepdene railway stations. Housebuilding was further encouraged by the faster and more frequent train service which followed electrification of the railway to Epsom and London, carried out in two stages, in 1925 and 1929.

From 1921, Maurice Chance, entrepreneur, property developer, insurance assessor and urban district councillor, set about developing the Deepdene Park Estate in informal style with detached three, four and five-bedroom houses spaced two, three or four to the acre, designed to attract the more affluent commuters and local professionals. These and similar houses on the former Denbies (Bradley Farm) lands were within easy walking distance of the main railway station, as were the smaller detached houses built from 1924 on A. B. Apted's land at the east side of Deepdene Avenue and in Deepdene Avenue Road. Adjoining this, Chance's Deepdene Vale development, started in 1926, was of a similar, railway-oriented nature with direct footpath access to the stations. Of the six or seven small estates of more modest and mostly semi-detached houses of typical suburban design built in the late 1920s and the 1930s, only one was at all close to Dorking North station. Given the higher season ticket rates and the large number of similarly priced new houses then available much nearer London, it seems likely that these Dorking semis were taken mostly by people working in the town rather than commuters.

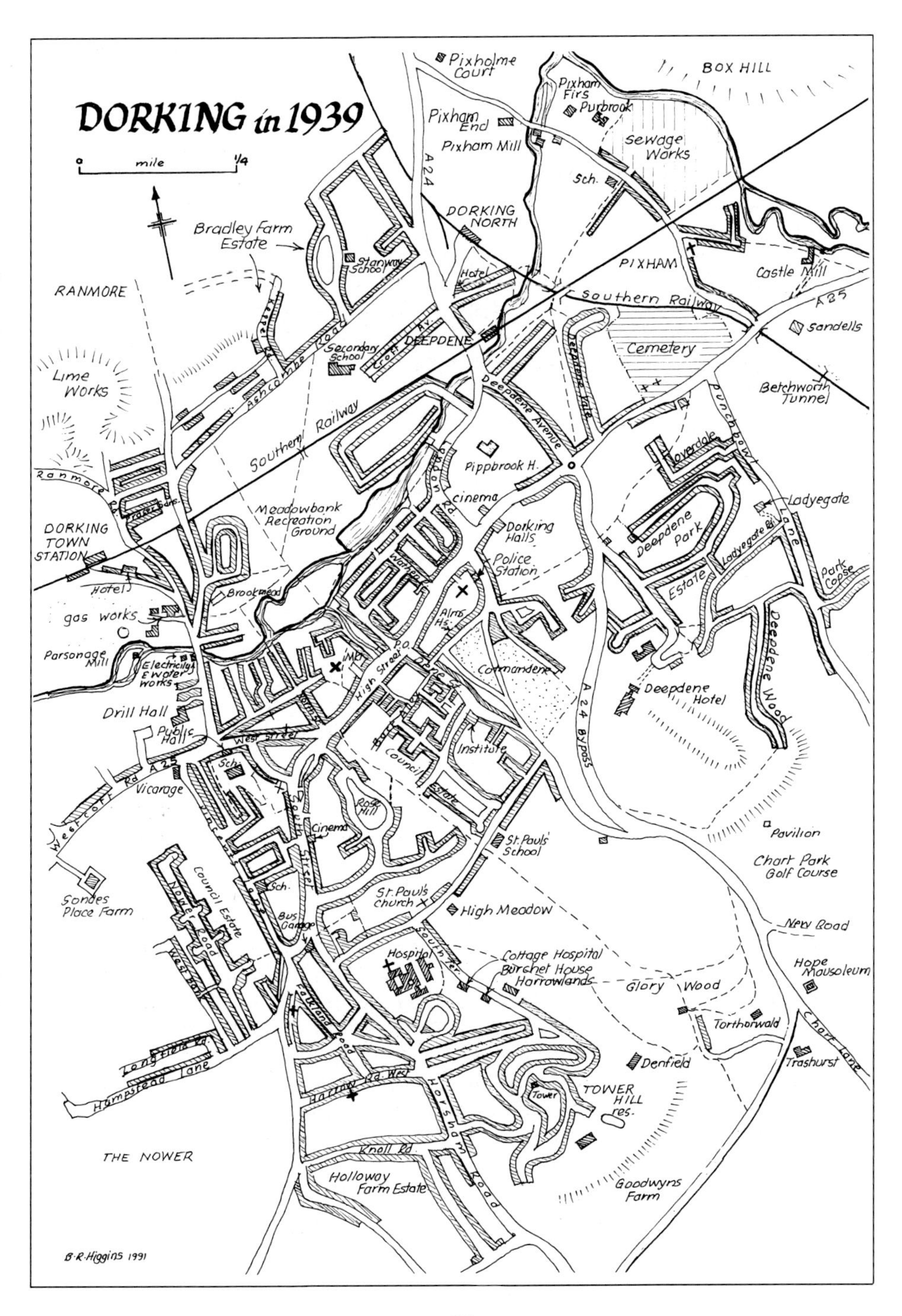
DORKING in 1939
0 mile 1/4
Pixholme Court
BOX HILL
Pixham Firs
Purbrook
Pixham End
Pixham Mill
Sewage Works
A24
Sch.
DORKING NORTH
Bradley Farm Estate
Stanway School
Hotel
PIXHAM
Castle Mill
RANMORE
Southern Railway
A25
Sandells
Secondary School
Croft Av.
DEEPDENE
Cemetery
Ashcombe Road
Keppel Rd.
Lime Works
Deepdene Avenue
Deepdene Vale
Betchworth Tunnel
Punchbowl
Southern Railway
Pippbrook H.
Coverdale
Ranmore Rd.
cinema
Ladyegate
Meadowbank Recreation Ground
Dorking Halls
Deepdene Park
Ladyegate Rd.
DORKING TOWN STATION
Police Station
Estate
Lane
Park Copse
Hotel
Brookmead
Alms Hs.
Deepdene Wood
gas works
Parsonage Mill
Electricity & water works
P.O.
High Street
Cotmandene
Deepdene Hotel
Drill Hall
A24 By pass
Public Hall
West Street
Council
Institute
Sch.
A25
Estate
Westcott Rd.
Vicarage
Rose Hill
Cinema
Pavilion
St. Pauls' School
Chart Park Golf Course
Sondes Place Farm
Council Estate
Nower Road
Sch.
South Street
St. Paul's Church
High Meadow
New Road
Bus Garage
Hospital
Cottage Hospital
Burchet House
Harrowlands
Glory Wood
Hope Mausoleum
West Bank
Falkland Road
Torthorwald
Chart Lane
Longfield Rd.
Humpstead Lane
Denfield
Trashurst
Harrow Rd. West
Horsham Road
Tower
TOWER HILL res.
Knoll Rd.
THE NOWER
Holloway Farm Estate
Goodwyns Farm
B·R·Higgins 1991

When the Dorking UDC Town Planning Scheme was confirmed in 1939, the built-up area extended over 412 acres with a population of around 17,300, but the Scheme boldly proposed an additional 1,000 acres of development with an eventual total population of 80,000. This would have produced an urban/suburban sprawl, merging Dorking town with Westcott, Westhumble, Brockham and North Holmwood, a circumstance mercifully prevented by the outbreak of war and the 1947 Town & Country Planning Act. After World War 2, residential growth was severely restricted by the Green Belt ring around the town and the shortage of suitable sites within it, a situation which led to vigorous 'infilling'* at Tower Hill and elsewhere. Abandoned industrial sites were also used for residential purposes: in 1983-89 the Dorking Brick Company's works between Inholms Lane and the Bentsbrook was cleared and covered with small houses in a somewhat cramped suburban type layout; and two other developments, Masons' Paddock (1966–67) and Ranmore Park (1988) made use of the old chalkpits north of Ranmore Road. Hospital lands around South Terrace provided another opportunity to raise residential density in 1988–89, at the cost of some damage to the beauty of the approaches to Glory Wood, given to the town in 1929 by the Duke of Newcastle.

Most of the post-1950 private housing was located to the south west of the town and at North Holmwood, the latter by 1970 virtually a suburb of Dorking. Availability of the motor car to all but the lowest income groups, and the dispersal of job opportunities away from central London meant that distance from the main railway station was no longer as important as it had been in the 1920s and 1930s.

Council Housing

Operating under central government legislation directed at increasing the national housing stock immediately after World War 1, the Dorking UDC built its first estate at Nower Road (98 houses) in 1920–21. Locally-based firms were given contracts and for some, such as G. J. Arthur & Sons and A. & P. Clear, it proved a valuable opportunity to gain experience and enhance their reputation. Next came Back Alley/ Marlborough Road (50 houses, 1925–26), then Beresford Road (Poultry Farm)) (1927–28, 80 houses). All of this was conscientious but dreadfully dull design by S. S. Gettings, the UDC Engineer & Surveyor, but the 1937 Fraser Gardens (30 houses), on land bought from the Denbies Estate with money donated by Sir Malcolm and Lady Fraser of Pixholme Court, benefited from the attention of the eminent architect G. Grey Wornum, brought in by Sir Malcolm.

---

* Planners' jargon for increasing density by erecting groups of houses or apartment blocks on plots formerly occupied by one large Victorian or Edwardian house and its extensive grounds.

In 1936, after obtaining Slum Clearance Orders, the UDC made a determined attack on old cottage housing, demolishing 81 insanitary and inadequate properties in Church and North Streets, Spring Gardens, Cotmandene Square, Heath Hill, Mill Lane and Horsham Road. Altogether 217 people were rehoused, 173 by the UDC, mostly at Fraser Gardens and at another new estate in Watson's Road, Westcott (1935–36). By 1940 the UDC had erected 345 houses on 34 acres, accommodating some 1,500.

Delayed by the war, a second round of clearance of substandard housing was accomplished in 1945–64, affecting some 140 properties, mainly in Lincoln and Orchard Roads, Dene Street, Church Gardens and Hampstead and Falkland Roads. Demolitions of individual cottages continued for another ten years or so after these clusters had been dealt with.

A commendably vigorous public housing programme was carried through between 1947 and 1980 against the background of a housing list that at times exceeded 900 families, but in its execution, the Council paid scant regard to the special environmental value of the town and its outskirts. One exception to this was the 1953 Chequers Place, a pleasing grouping of 20 small white-walled houses around a green near Rose Hill to the designs of the locally-resident architect, Donald H. McMorran. The first postwar development was the 1948–52 Chart Downs estate, between the Deepdene Avenue By-pass and the southern part of Chart Lane, providing 183 housing units on a green field site so remote from the town that it has required its own bus service ever since.

But the Council's major exercise in the housing field was the controversial Goodwyns Farm Estate. Substantially completed in 1960, this was initially designed by Clifford Culpin and later by William W. Ryder. With remarkable insensitivity, two uncompromisingly urban 120 ft, 14-storey tower blocks designed by Ryder were imposed on this Green Belt site in 1964, creating a precedent for Surrey. Goodwyns provided a total of 637 housing units strewn below the wooded escarpment which had until then provided a fine vista for the southern approaches to the town. Its 44 acres were secured in 1952 by compulsory purchase order from Howard Martineau, a major benefactor to Dorking for some thirty years, in the teeth of his fierce opposition. He died a year later, no doubt a very sad man.

From the late 1970s the public housing contribution showed greater sensitivity to the scale of its surroundings, not conflicting as harshly as before with older buildings or with its scenic background. This can be seen at the 1978 Lyon's Court (42 units), the 1983 Chapel Court, Church Street (50 units) and the 1987 Archway Place (26 units).

More Schools

Population growth generated a demand for new school buildings. In 1931 the co-educational Dorking County School was completed in Ashcombe Road to replace the two inadequate High Schools. Thirty years later, its roll had reached 625. Mowbray County Secondary Modern, for 450 girls, was opened nearby in September 1959 and the two buildings were combined in autumn 1975 to form a Comprehensive, now known as Ashcombe School.

After World War 2, construction of new school buildings was actively pursued by the County Council: Powell Corderoy County Primary and Middle Schools were rehoused in Longfield Road in 1968 and St. Martin's Middle School at Ranmore Road in 1969, where it was joined by the First School in 1985. A County Secondary Modern Mixed School started life in 1947, at first using the Chart Lane Institute and hutments in Longfield Road. Permanent buildings for 660 boys were opened at the latter site in 1960 and 1969, in what was then to become known as the Sondes Place School. The large Goodwyns Estate and neighbouring developments justified Primary (1955) and Middle (1957) Schools, with a total roll of 400.

Dorking continued to provide fertile ground for private education. There were over a dozen private schools in the area in 1960, including Stanway (originally Oak Tree), based in a purpose-built complex between Calvert and Chichester Roads which had opened in 1934, only to require extension in 1936 and again in 1939.

Hospitals: Growth and Decline

Dorking Hospital had evolved from the 1841 General Mixed Workhouse of the Dorking Union and the adjacent Poor Law Infirmary of 1901, these buildings (which still survive) becoming a County Hospital in 1936 and an NHS General Hospital in 1948. The nearby Cottage Hospital, which had been further enlarged and modernised in 1926 to accommodate a total of 23 beds and a children's ward, became known as the Dorking & District Voluntary Hospital in 1919 and was amalgamated with the former County Hospital to form the Dorking General Hospital after the introduction of the National Health Service in 1948. The old Cottage Hospital building was pulled down in 1986, its site sold off for development as private residential flats (The Pines). The rest ceased to be a true local resource as its valued services were drastically curtailed in the early 1990s in favour of concentration at the East Surrey Hospital, Redhill.

Dorking emerged from the 19th century the only area in Surrey without an isolation hospital for infectious patients, fierce resistance having been mounted by the UDC on the dubious grounds that the town's health record made such an image-damaging extravagance unnecessary. After statutory powers had been obtained, Surrey County Council imposed its will, requiring a hospital shared with the Rural District Council. This was duly provided on a 4-acre site at Logmore Lane, Westcott, initially with 22 beds. Opening in 1902 to receive mostly scarlet fever and diphtheria cases, it was extended and improved in 1910 and 1923. Seriously damaged by a German missile in 1944, it was closed and converted to residential accommodation ten years later.

Motor Traffic Makes its Mark

As they gazed in bewilderment at the sight of the first motor car passing through the town on 27 November 1896, few if any bystanders could have guessed at the changes the newcomer would require in a small town astride two important trunk roads merging to share its High Street. As early as 1904, some 200 cars were passing through on summer Sundays and with some Sabbatarian reluctance voiced, the UDC agreed

The new Dorking East By-pass (now the A24) cuts across the front of Deepdene House. Looking north, 1934. *Postcard. (Alan A. Jackson).*

to call out the water cart to lay the dust they stirred up. About 1909 tar spraying and gritting was started as an alternative to summer watering. By the end of the 1920s, the newly-tarmacadamed main streets had become seriously congested, a contemporary writer remarking that the High Street was 'as reposeful as Piccadilly in the afternoon'. On fine Sundays, the through traffic created near intolerable conditions, severely taxing Dorking's 13-man police force.

A by-pass was inevitably projected, the route it should take stirring up a major controversy. Although many argued for a more logical course around the then undeveloped north and west sides of the town, which would also have relieved the east-west traffic flow through the congested centre, central government and County Council saw to it that the new road (now the A24, Deepdene Avenue) took the cheapest route in money terms, ruthlessly carving through the beautiful Deepdene Park in 1931–34. Thirty years later (1965) the northern section between Pixham Lane and the Reigate Road roundabout was uglified into a dual carriageway, a sad contrast to the pretty double avenue of limes up to Deepdene House that had existed here until 1931.

In the town itself, South Street was widened out at its northern end in 1920–21, works planned since 1905 and carried out with UDC and county funds as a contribution to the relief of unemployment. Picturesque if dilapidated old houses and shops on the east side were demolished, but there was some consideration for the townscape, the widening incorporating a bandstand (provided by a private benefactor) and a war memorial. Although new building lines were prescribed between the wars, and subsequent new structures were set back, the local authorities were inhibited from further central area widenings on the South Street scale by the heavy cost of compensation such work would entail. Declaration of South Street, West Street and High Street as a Conservation Area in 1974 effectively stopped further consideration of wholesale destruction of this kind.

By the 1930s, the noise of motor vehicles in South Street had rendered it almost impossible for the Town Band to continue to use the bandstand which it had welcomed with such enthusiasm. The weight of motor traffic in the High Street had also caused the Monday live stock market to be moved from the cobblestones to the yard behind the Three Tuns. Generous provision was made in this new 1926 market for cattle stallage, sheep and pig pens, poultry cages and egg sales.

Dorking had a narrow escape from further major devastation in the interests of motor traffic. Around 1950, County Council planners, spurning local consultation, produced a scheme for a dual carriageway 'inner relief road' with large roundabouts at each end. This would have cut up the town severely on the north side of the High Street, completely destroying much of its character and scale and isolating the northern district from the town centre. The scheme remained a live issue for three decades, arousing understandable resentment and protest whilst the council purchased properties along the route. Fortunately the opening of the M25 in 1985, combined with improvements to the A3, led to a perceptible reduction in the flow of east-west traffic through the town centre, and by 1982, with this in prospect, the relief road scheme was dead.

Pressure of local car use brought about further change in the 1960s and 1970s including prohibition of main street parking and provision of pay car parks, which sterilised and uglified many valuable sites. A one way system for South Street, Vincent Lane and West Street was introduced in 1968 and in the following year traffic wardens arrived to enforce parking regulations.

Rise and Decline of the Motor Bus

One great benefit of the new motor age was the proliferation of bus services after 1920, vastly improving communications between Dorking and its surrounding rural communities. The first enduring regular services

Dorking High Street looking east, 1919. Red Lion Hotel right, London 'General' motor bus on service 107 (later 70) from Clapham Common approaching. *Postcard. (John Coombes).*

began in 1914 under three operators: East Surrey Traction Co (Redhill – Dorking); Aldershot & District Traction Co (Leatherhead – Dorking – Guildford*); and the London General Omnibus Co (Clapham Common – Dorking). The latter ran only on Saturdays and Sundays until 1916, when the buses began to run daily; its open-top double deckers brought huge crowds into town at fine weekends, providing regular amusement for Dorkinians, who gathered to watch the sometimes tipsy trippers struggling on to their homebound buses.

Expansion of bus services was rapid in the 1920s, and in 1932 a 40-vehicle garage, with a 15-vehicle bus station in its forecourt, was opened on the site of a house called Townfield, at the junction of South Street and Horsham Road. Here, at least, some attempt was made to

---

* From December 1916 this service ran only between Dorking and Guildford

provide a motor age building with a pleasing frontage. From 1930, in addition to the local services, half hourly limited-stop Green Line coaches began to operate between Dorking and central London.

With the drastic loss of patronage which followed the wide spread of car ownership after the 1950s, cuts were made, but some loss-making routes were retained with the help of central and local government subsidies, made available from 1971. By the 1980s, local buses were frequently seen running around almost empty, their few passengers confined to the old, schoolchildren, and the car-less minority. Direct Green Line coach services to London were withdrawn in 1987, their residual traffic abandoned to the railway. With bus 'de-regulation', smaller vehicles appeared, some on new routes, but sale of assets seemed to become as, if not more, important than public service, and the garage and bus station, together with its information and booking office, was summarily closed in 1990.

The Town at War

Dorking was not greatly affected by World War 1, apart that is from the tragic human sacrifice, duly recorded on the South Street memorial. At Denbies there was much sorrow at this time; Henry, the second Baron Ashcombe (1867–1947) lost his three eldest sons, whose deaths are commemorated at St. Barnabas in a beautiful chapel, decorated with murals by E. Reginald Frampton.

Large numbers of troops were stationed in and around the town and empty shops and houses were requisitioned by the military. Amongst war workers seen in the streets were the Forestry Corps, busily engaged in stripping the adjacent hill country of its standing timber. Other temporary residents appeared. A sharp series of air raids on London in the summer of 1917 produced around 2,000 refugees, arriving by train and the Clapham bus to seek accommodation in a town already full of summer visitors. A local newspaper declared they were 'for the most part East End Jews' and noted that so overcrowded was the town, some were obliged to sleep in the open air.

World War 2 provided rather more drama. Men of the British Army withdrawn through Dunkerque in June 1940 passed through on the east-west railway, waved and cheered on their way by the townspeople. Empty properties again provided billets for the armed forces, British and Canadian. During 1940, the threat of German invasion was very strongly felt in the town, many no doubt recalling the fictional Battle of Dorking mentioned earlier. Indeed the authorities did plan for such a defensive stand before London, with some householders being warned their property might have to be vacated at very short notice and demolished, as it was in a line of fire. Many defensive positions and tank obstacles were planned and prepared, the enthusiastic local contingent of the Home Guard playing an important role.

It is recorded that 77 high-explosive bombs and 60 incendiaries were dropped on the town by the Luftwaffe, but there was remarkably little damage to property and few casualties. The only incident in the town involving fatalities occurred at Fraser Gardens on 29 October 1940 when two women and a girl were killed and two houses were demolished, with others damaged.

In 1938 a refugee committee was formed to help those arriving from Europe before hostilities began and many were accommodated in the area. Over 3,000 South London schoolchildren and mothers with babies were evacuated by train to the Dorking district in September 1939. Many soon went home, only to return in autumn 1940 when the blitz started. Several London firms set up wartime offices in and around the town, the most notable being the Southern Railway at Deepdene and Henley Cables at Milton Court.

Eclipse of the Old Estates

The new century saw dramatic changes to the three large estates around the edge of the town. Following the breaking up of the Hope properties in 1920–21, the Deepdene mansion with its historic garden leading up to the Terrace became a country hotel. Its attractions as such were soon enough severely damaged by the wound of the by-pass, which swept close below its north west front, and in 1939 the owners must have been relieved they could sell it to the Southern Railway Company, seeking a 'safe area' headquarters to control its wartime operations. Railway staff stayed on here until 1966, by which time the fabric was very badly affected by dry and wet rot. In these circumstances it was a fairly easy task for the developers who purchased the mansion in 1967 to obtain permission for demolition. Council planners alleged that the wartime office use made it difficult to refuse consent for a new office building, and two low profile blocks in Modern Style white architecture by E. C. Percy were erected on the site of the mansion and stable block in 1971–72, totally out of keeping with their parkland surroundings. With them came the inevitable approach roads and car parks, the latter made by concreting over the lower part of the once beautiful gardens. The rest of the Deepdene gardens were left to nature and lie today neglected, decayed and overgrown, public access denied. Fortunately the terrace above the gardens was secured for the enjoyment of the public in 1943 by the Dorking & Leith Hill District Preservation Society, though sadly this too was not adequately maintained by the Council.

The greater part of the Denbies estate remained in the hands of the Lords Ashcombe, life for a time continuing much as before. In 1934 there was still an indoor staff of 24. Between 1926 and 1939 some of the land near the town was developed as a middle class building estate (Ashcombe, Chichester, Calvert, Yew Tree and Keppel Roads) with houses priced at £2,600 to £3,250.* Building was resumed in 1950, but an attempt to complete the northern section of Keppel Road was squashed by the planning authorities in 1954.

Impossible to operate economically in contemporary conditions, the enormous and (in truth) ugly Cubitt mansion was demolished in 1953. Following the death of the second Lord Ashcombe (1867–1947), the third, Roland (1899–1962) had converted the estate laundry and stablemen's and gardeners' quarters into a modern residence for himself. Shortly afterwards, some 800 acres of the estate passed to the National Trust and in 1984, the 4th Lord put the remainder on the market. The purchasers were the locally-based water treatment firm of Biwater, whose chairman, Adrian White occupied and enlarged the 1950s house and quickly proceeded to develop much of the land as Britain's largest vineyard.

In the hands of the Barclays, the Quaker brewing family, since 1805, the 969 acre Bury Hill estate had been the subject of an unsuccessful sale in 1914. Its last occupant was Lt. Col. R. W. Barclay (1880–1951), chairman of Barclay, Perkins & Co, brewers, who vacated it to the military in 1940, severing the long connection. After World War 2, the 18th century mansion was sold for conversion to residential apartments and during this work, in October 1949, the central part was destroyed by a serious fire. Most of the rest of the estate was split up and sold off in 1952 to pay Col. Barclay's death duties.

Against 'injurious changes'

Alarmed by 'injurious changes already inflicted or threatened', a group of public-spirited individuals formed the Dorking & Leith Hill District Preservation Society in 1929 'with the general object of watching developments in the district and safeguarding its rural character'. This was too late to do much about the Deepdene By-pass road, and was alas unable to stop the tower blocks at Goodwyns and other post war municipal and commercial uglification, nor could it do anything to arrest the decay, demolition and neglect of Deepdene and its gardens. Nevertheless, the Society has many commendable achievements to its credit. In 1989 it adopted the shorter title of the Dorking & District Preservation Society and continued to be vigilant, regularly reviewing planning applications. It fostered a museum, opened in West Street in 1976 and a Local History Group, founded in 1967.

Public services further improved

Development and growth of public utilities and services continued into the first decades of the new century. Edmundson's Electricity

---

* At the time the average cost of a suburban semi was £600–£700.

Corporation, leasing an undertaking owned by the UDC, started supplying 100 consumers with direct current (dc) from a new works in Station Road in 1904, using two 90kW generators driven by steam engines. By 1926 there were 975 consumers and two years later, the UDC having discovered it would be cheaper, electric street lighting replaced gas. Electricity supply became the responsibility of the Home Counties Joint Electricity Authority in 1931, from which time supplies were taken from the National Grid, although dc was not finally eliminated in the town centre until 1957.

1928 saw the merger of the Dorking and Redhill Gas Companies to form the East Surrey Gas Co, after which mains were linked up. The site in Station Road continued to expand, taking in more land in 1930 and again in 1937, when the 7-acre Taylor & Brooker timber works was acquired. In the event the latter was used only for coke storage and no further extension of the gas making plant was undertaken, production of town gas in Dorking ceasing towards the end of 1956.

The Dorking Water Company, which had at last ensured adequate supplies by establishing new boreholes and a steam-powered pumping plant in Station Road in 1904, long outlived the gas undertaking, not merging into the East Surrey Water Company until January 1959. Today the town's water is no longer entirely local in origin, some coming from the River Eden in distant Kent.

The Volunteer Fire Brigade became a full time affair in 1912, under the direct control of the UDC, which purchased its first motor fire engine in 1921. Nine years later, the town brigade took over from the volunteer units which had served the satellite villages, extending its commitments over 25 square miles and acquiring a second motor appliance. A motor ambulance, operated since 1921 by a voluntary committee, became a Council responsibility in 1936, in which year a second vehicle was provided by voluntary subscription. These vehicles and their crews were accommodated in the West Street Public Hall building, which was purchased by the Council in 1934 to be specially adapted for the purpose. Following transfer to Surrey County Council control in 1948, new facilities were erected at North Holmwood in 1971, placing the fire, rescue and ambulance services conveniently close to the main roads leading directly to most parts of the town and its environs.

Leak problems still persisting, the swimming bath in Station Road was closed in June 1939 when a daily total of 10,000 gallons was seeping away. Much-needed replacement facilities finally became available in December 1974 in the form of the Dorking Swimming Centre, Reigate Road, a featureless, low-profile Modern style building by John Rice and D. S. Roberts.

Telephone service was first provided by the National Telephone Company, whose exchange at High Street/Mill Lane opened in August 1900.

When the Post Office took over in 1912, the exchange was transferred to 11, Rose Hill which in 1921 was hardly overworked by the 197 subscribers. Customer numbers had grown to 643 by 1932 and in 1935, with 900, the exchange moved into the new Post Office building in the High Street, where there was accommodation for 4,800 lines, a capacity still not reached in 1960, when there were 3,543 subscribers. However the demand was still rising and in 1965 a new exchange was opened at London Road/Reigate Road, with an extension following in 1977. The local system was fully automated in December 1981, and further modernised in 1991.

Making the most of Meadowbank

During 1926 the UDC bought the house called Meadowbank and its 29 acres of land, the intention being to use the property partly as a recreation ground and partly for 150 further council houses. There were second thoughts about the financial burden of the latter, and eventually this section was purchased by Maurice Chance, who sold on to A. F. Davis, a London speculative builder. Davis erected Parkway, an estate of modest semi-detached houses, in 1934–35, advertising them and his neighbouring Chalkpit Lane semis at £475 to £695. Like others of their kind on the edges of the town, many of these inexpensive houses enjoyed superb views.

The new recreation ground, the town's first, was landscaped and completed at a leisurely pace between 1930 and 1940. It incorporated the 1894 Willow Walk and the old Pippbrook mill pond, whose malodorous state and use as a rubbish dump continued to be the source of periodical complaints. Once part of the Denbies estate, the millpond was given to the town in 1934 by Chance, who had purchased it with the land to the north which he developed in 1935–39 with small houses as Fairfield Drive.

After 1953, Meadowbank in its new guise also provided a permanent home for Dorking Football Club, long known as 'The Chicks' after the five-clawed Dorking breed of poultry. This bird was incorporated in the DUDC seal in 1894, in its coat of arms of 1951 and in the Mole Valley Council arms of 1975. The 'Five-clawed 'Un' was also widely adopted by local firms and organisations as well as decorating road signs at the entrance to the town.

More for Local Government

Another estate close to Meadowbrook also saw change. Pippbrook ceased to be a private residence in 1928 and the Victorian house, with 5.75 acres of its grounds, was eventually purchased by the UDC, which moved its offices there from South Street in December 1931. Council meetings were held in the converted 1858 ballroom from March 1932.

A public library, staffed by the Rotary Club, and lacking a reference department, was provided in a room beneath the Council Chamber in 1934; full time library facilities did not appear until 1949.

In 1928 Surrey's smallest urban district was allowed to increase its area from 1,339 to 1,728 acres by absorbing Pixham and other sites on the town fringes. But this was as nothing compared to the 'Greater Dorking' created by the Surrey Review Order of 1933, which gave the UDC responsibility from 1 April for a total of 9,511 acres and a population approaching 16,000, bringing into its governance Brockham, Mickleham, North Holmwood and Westcott. In the ensuing six years, the Council devoted much effort to supplying modern main drainage facilities to Mickleham, Westhumble, Westcott and North Holmwood, expenditure which benefited private housebuilders.

In 1974, with reorganisation of local government, the town found itself part of a new 'Mole Valley District' of 63,837 acres, a combination of the old Dorking and Leatherhead Urban Districts and the eleven parishes of the former Dorking & Horley Rural District. This covered a population of around 77,000 in 1990.

Rationalisation of council accommodation followed, the almost central position of Dorking within the new boundaries ensuring its choice as the administrative centre. To accommodate officers and council chamber, the Norwich architect Michael Innes produced a pleasing and slightly whimsical low profile complex of interconnected pavilions in warm red brick and matching tiles. Opened in 1984, the new Pippbrook

The 1984 Mole Valley District Council Offices, Pippbrook, Reigate Road, looking north, 1991. *Photograph Alan A. Jackson.*

offices were arguably the most successful piece of post-war architecture in the town until that time, though initially scorned by the more conservative element. The 1856 mansion, its beautiful Victorian interior skilfully restored, was reopened in 1986 as a public library and social services centre.

Lost Cinemas

The Reigate Road site of the new council offices had associations with a potent form of twentieth century entertainment. The landscaped car park provided for the new building, happily opening up views towards Ranmore, was on the site of the Embassy, Dorking's most modern and largest cinema. Designed by Harry Weston, with accommodation for 1,290, this had opened as the Gaumont in 1938 and after its closure as a cinema in 1973, had served as a meeting place for Jehovah's Witnesses until its demolition in 1983.

Films had first been shown in the town on a regular basis from 1910, in the old Dorking Club building in Club Court, on the south side of the High Street, and now used by the Salvation Army. A rudimentary facility, with wooden benches and narrow (often crowded) aisle, the first picture house was a fearsome fire-hazard, masquerading under the totally undeserved title of the Cinema Royal. It closed soon after World

High Street looking west, 1938. Dorking Halls at left. In the foreground an example of the elegant lamp standards provided for the electrification of street lighting in 1927. *Postcard (John Coombes).*

War 1, overtaken by the 1913 Royal Electric Cinema (later New Electric and then the Regent), built in the garden of Stapleton House in South Street. This survived in its intended role until 1938. A third cinema, The Pavilion, erected in 1925 a little further south along the same street, continued to show films until 1963. It still stands, currently in use as a building supplies store. Both Regent and Pavilion were converted to show talkies, but only silent films were screened at a fifth location, the

Public Hall, West Street, which from 1919 until early in 1930 operated as a cinema under the banner of 'The Playhouse'.

Vaughan Williams and the Dorking Halls

Entertainment and culture were also available at the Dorking Halls in the Reigate Road, at the eastern end of the town. Designed by Percy W. Meredith and opened in January 1931, these three interconnected halls with a frontage vaguely suggestive of seaside architecture, were to serve the community well for a great variety of social, entertainment and business purposes, but achieved wide fame from their long association with the music and musical activities of the town's most celebrated 20th century resident, the composer Ralph Vaughan Williams OM (1872–1958). At the Leith Hill Musical Competitions and Festival, founded in 1905 by Lady Farrer of Abinger Hall and Vaughan Williams' sister Margaret, VW acted as conductor and many of his new compositions were first performed. He lived at White Gates, Westcott Road (now demolished) from 1929 to 1953, taking an active interest in community affairs. The Halls were built and financed by a private local company in which Vaughan Williams, Howard Martineau and the Duke of Newcastle were much involved. Their enterprise proved something of a financial disaster and in 1946 the building was purchased by the UDC at a price well below the 1931 outlay.

The Built Environment since 1950

For thirty years or so after World War 2 the town, like many others of its kind, suffered from unworthy new buildings which had a negative or worse visual effect, whatever benefits they might have brought to its economy. It is of course true that the architectural style of this period was often dreary, and frequently ugly, but the overall result of the planning consents reflected little credit on the aesthetic taste and imagination of the majority of local councillors, who until 1962 preferred to be without professional architectural advice on planning applications for sensitive sites and were only too ready to allow historic buildings to be demolished rather than restored.

Whilst there was considerable modernisation of retail premises, most of the new construction was to increase office jobs. Somewhat concealed by trees, the featureless barracks of the Friends' Provident and Century Assurance on a 43-acre site at Pixham End on the London Road, just north of the main station, were completed in 1957, to the designs of F. Leslie Preston and John M. Easton. With their pitched and coppered roof lines offered in self-conscious atonement for their cheeky appropriation of an attractive and prominent woodland site at the foot of Box Hill, these offices eventually accommodated some 800 staff, making their owners the largest employers in the town.

Less concealed, though well set back from the same road, Federated House, an office block immediately north of Deepdene station, was allowed only after an appeal to the Minister. This grim, flat-roofed building of 1965 intruded most unhappily into all the distant views of the Mole Gap from the Deepdene, Denbies, the Glory, Cotmandene, Box Hill or Pixham, offering clear testimony that planners of the period paid no regard to sight lines. With these two sets of offices in position, it was inevitable more would follow in the same area, as they did in 1981, 1987 and 1989.

Dorking from Box Hill, 1991. The tower crane used for construction of the St. Martin's Walk development can be seen immediately in front of the Parish Church. In the right foreground, the 1965 Federated House. *Photograph John Day.*

A little further south Sir John Soane's 1780 Punchbowl Inn in Reigate Road was completely rebuilt inside in 1971 and given an annexe in the form of a 29-bedroom two-storey motor hotel. To hide the somewhat functional outlines of the latter from view, especially from Box Hill, the Preservation Society obtained agreement that an artificial mound and trees should be placed in front of it, and with the passing of time, it became suitably obscured.

In 1960–1 and again in 1973, great visual damage was perpetrated in South Street by inserting a series of starkly plain retail and office buildings into the homely 18th and 19th century frontages on both sides of the road south of the Spotted Dog. This was indeed a low period; the Ram Inn at the corner of Dene Street was pulled down in 1959, and the historic Red Lion Inn, which had closed for business in that year was most regrettably demolished in 1964, to be replaced by a characterless block of five shops with flats above.

Towards the end of the 1970s, things began to improve; the old Gun and Wheatsheaf Inns were saved and restored, and more care was given to the design and siting of new buildings. The Magistrates' Court moved into new premises north of Pippbrook in 1979, dropped low into the plot to respect sight lines. The vacated 1894 courthouse and police station in the High Street was demolished in 1986, except for the police superintendent's house. In its place, Michael Lyell Associates provided an agreeable Neo-Vernacular office block with a small clock tower.

At the western end of the town, the long- established light industrial areas on the west side of Station Road and Vincent Lane were further developed in the 1960s and 1970s, the former including the site of the old Parsonage Mill. Five and a half acres of the abandoned gasworks site in Station Road were sold in 1982, to be converted in 1989 to the 'Dorking Business Park', an interesting grouping of nine Post-Modernist office buildings. Further south along Station Road, nearer the town centre, the site of the former H. G. Kingham grocery warehouse and the Girl's High School was rebuilt in 1987–88 as Parsonage Square, a series of five self-contained office blocks, including a handsome restoration of the Victorian house once the home of the School. To the north of this, Canterbury Court, a pleasant Neo-Vernacular block of 46 flats for retired people, was completed early in 1989.

Dorking at the end of the Twentieth Century

As the town entered the last decade of the century, the high level of activity in new construction, especially of office building, appeared at last to be tailing-off. Most residents did not welcome the possibility of further major changes in the built environment and there was increasing concern about the appearance of new work and its relationship to existing frontages and the surrounding areas of high landscape quality.

The century had witnessed a transformation from a comfortable, quiet country market town, not into yet another dormitory suburb of London as some had once expected, but into a largely self-sufficient business, residential, tourist and specialist retail centre, with London commuters very much in the minority amongst its inhabitants. Despite the impact of many changes and social upheavals since 1901, Dorking still exhibited a tangible independence from the metropolis, its citizens increasingly sensitive about the still numerous reminders of an even-tenored past. Well integrated, with a strong sense of place, the town continued to fulfil its historic role as a focal point for the villages in its beautiful rural surroundings.

St. Martin's Square, the central feature of the 1991 St. Martin's Walk shopping development. *Drawing by John Watson (Bredero Dorking Ltd.).*

APPENDIX

Population

1801	Town area	3,058
1811	Town area	3,259
1851	Town area	3,490
1861	Town area	4,061
1871	Town area	5,419
....		
1881	Local Board Area (1,340 acres)	6,328
1891	Local Board Area (1,340 acres)	7,132
1901	UDC Area (1,340 acres)	7,670
1911	UDC Area (1,340 acres)	7,848
1921	UDC Area (1,340 acres)	8,518
....		
1921	UDC Area as enlarged 1933 (9,511 acres) (1)	13,207
1931	UDC Area as enlarged 1933 (9,511 acres)	15,204
1938	UDC Area as enlarged 1933 (9,511 acres) (2)	17,110
....		
1947	UDC Area (9,573 acres) (3)	20,460
1951	UDC Area (9,573 acres)	20,252
1961	UDC Area (9,573 acres)	22,594
1971	UDC Area (9,573 acres)	22,354
....		

NOTES: All figures except 1938 and 1947 are from the Census Returns. Figures between the dotted lines are comparable since they relate to exactly the same area. Figures in first two sections (1801–1921) are only broadly comparable.

(1) From here onwards figures include Pixham (part of UDC since 1928), also Brockham, Mickleham, and North Holmwood (part of UDC since 1933)

(2) Mid-year estimate by Medical Officer of Health

(3) Mid-year estimate by Medical Officer of Health

SOURCES AND SELECT BIBLIOGRAPHY

Abbreviations:

DLHG	Dorking Local History Group
DM	Dorking & District Museum
Ed	Editor
nd	no date
SAC	Surrey Archaeological Collections
SAS	Surrey Archaeological Society
SCC	Surrey County Council
SRO	Surrey Record Office
SRS	Surrey Record Society

PRINCIPAL SOURCES

1. Arundel Castle Archives: Manor of Dorking: surveys, accounts, court rolls and other documents.
2. Hampshire Record Office: Bishops' Registers.
3. Ordnance Survey Map, One Inch to One Mile, Old Series, 1816.
4. Ordnance Survey Maps, 25 inches to one mile, various editions.
5. Public Record Office: Chancery, Exchequer and Probate records, Assize Rolls.
6. SAS: Hooper papers, O'Flahertie's transcripts of Manor of Dorking court rolls.
7. SRO (Kingston): Manor of Dorking 1649 survey, court rolls.
8. SRO (Guildford): Bray mss, Dorking parish registers.

SECONDARY SOURCES AND SELECT BIBLIOGRAPHY

Dorking & District Museum Collections:

9. Crow, F Lewis, typescript on the history of Dorking market, R 134 BP 2/1.
10. Crow's Property Registers R 134 BP 1/18/1–26.
11. Cuttings from local newspapers, 1869–1991: 10/DC series; 10/Balchin series; 10/Goldsmith series; 10/Scragg series; 10/White series; D & LHPS/series; 10 Gen/ series; Sellick collection O.SC 266/ 1,267,268,270,271.
12. *The Old Dorkinian,* Vol 1, No.1, November 1933, 'Early Days at the Girls' High School', 01/4.
13. Note on the *History of Dorking & District Hospital,* in programme of the First Hospital Carnival, 1932, SC E/3/8.
14. Beetham-Wilson, J, historical notes, *Dorking during the 1914-18 War,* SC 236/1.
15. Sellick, E. L, typescript of recollections, 1890-1950, SC H/4 (i) historical notes, SC H /1–21.

Publications:

16. *The Directory to Dorking, Leatherhead & District,* (Holmesdale Press), various years.
17. *Dorking Urban District Council, 1895–1974,* 1974.
18. *Kemp's Dorking and District Local Directory,* various years.
19. The Place Names of Surrey, English Place Name Society, vol 11, 1969.
20. SAC, 68, 185–6.
21. *Surrey Hearth Tax,* SRS, vol 17, 1940.
22. *Surrey Musters,* SRS, vols, 2, 10, 11, 13, 1914–20.
23. *Surrey Quarter Sessions Records,* SCC, 1934–38 (4 volumes).
24. *The 1235 Surrey Eyre,* SRS vols 31, 32, 1979 and 1983.
25. *Victoria County History of Surrey,* vol 3, 1911.

---

26. Andre, J. L., *Miscellaneous Antiquities of Dorking,* SAC 14.
27. Anon, *A History of J & W Attlee Ltd of Dorking,* nd c 1988.

28. Anon, *Mole Valley Official Guide,* various editions.

29. Aubrey, John, *The Natural History and Antiquities of Surrey,* 1719.

30. Bastian, F, *Daniel Defoe and the Dorking District,* SAC vol 55, 1957.

31. 'Bell Street', *East Surrey,* (A History of East Surrey bus services), 1974.

32. Bennett, Patricia, *Royal Occasions,* DLHG Newsletter (New Series), 8, 1988. 'Dorking History' (DLHG) 1, 1989.

33. Bennett, Patricia, and Sutton, Mary, *The Dorking Cock,* DLHG, 1985.

34. Bird, J, and Bird, D. G, (Eds) *The Archaeology of Surrey,* 1987.

35. Blair, John, *The Surrey Endowments of Lewes Priory before 1200,* SAC vol 72, 1980.

36. Brandon, P, *A History of Surrey,* 1977.

37. Brayley, E. W., *A Topographical History of Surrey,* vol 5, 1848.

38. Brigham, Allan, *Methodism in Dorking,* DLHG Newsletter (Old Series), 4, 5, 1976.

39. Bright, J. S., (a) *Dorking, A History of the Town with a Description of the Distinguished Residences....etc,* 1876
(b) *A History of Dorking and the Neighbouring Parishes,* 1884.

40. Carr, C. B.,*Dorking and its Solicitors before 1900,* DLHG Newsletter (Old Series) 3, 1975.

41. [Chesney, George, Tomkyns], *The Battle of Dorking: Reminiscences of a Volunteer,* 1871.

42. Clark, R. J., (publisher), *Walks, Rides & Drives Around Dorking: A Companionable Guide to the Neighbourhood, including Leatherhead,* various editions c 1873–1896.

43. Cole, Kenneth J, *Two Hundred Years of Dorking Cricket, 1766–1968,* 1969.

44. Course, Edwin, (Ed), *Minutes of the Board of Directors of the Reading, Guildford & Reigate Railway Company,* SRS vol 33, 1987.

45. Cousin, S, *The Dorking British School, 1816 to 1919,* 1919.

46. Defoe, Daniel, *A Tour through the Whole Island of Great Britain,* 1724.

47. [Dennis, John], *A Handbook of Dorking,* 1855.

48. Edwards, J, *Companion from London to Brighthelmston 1787,* 1801.

49. Edwards, Joan, *Dorothy Benson of Dorking: Pioneer Machine Embroiderer,* DLHG Newsletters (New Series) 6, 1987.

50. Elphick, Michael, *The Workhouse in Dorking before 1845,* DLHG Newsletters (Old Series) 13, 14, 15, 1981–82.
51. Ettlinger, Vivien, *Dorking at Domesday,* DLHG Newsletter (New Series), 4, 1986.
52. Ettlinger, Vivien, *The 1851 Census: A Window on Victorian Dorking,* 'Dorking History' (DLHG), 1, 1989.
53. Ettlinger, Vivien, *Not so Bright* (J. S. Bright DD), 'Dorking History' (DLHG), 5, 1991.
54. Foster, Joyce, *The 'Island' Site in South Street in 1851 and Later,* DLHG Newsletter (New Series) 7, 8, 1988.
55. Grantham, T. R, *Dorking Congregationalism 1662–1912 in Church, School and Village,* 1913.
56. Harrod, John, T. A., *Up The Dorking,* Parts 1 and 8, 'Southern Notebook, (Southern Railways Group) 83 (autumn 1984) and 90 (summer 1986).
57. Hearnshaw, F. J. C., *The Place of Surrey in the History of England,* 1936.
58. Higgins, Beryl and Ettlinger, Vivien, *Pilgrim Cottage, South Street, Dorking* 'Dorking History' (DLHG) 5, 1991.
59. Higgins, D., *The Thorntons of Dorking,* 1985.
60. Hillier, J., *Old Surrey Watermills,* 1951.
61. Hobhouse, Hermione, *Thomas Cubitt, Master Builder,* 1971.
62. Holland, Coffey, *Dorking People,* 1984.
63. Jackson, Alan A., *The Residential Development of Deepdene Park, Dorking, Since 1920,* DLHG, 1984.
64. Jackson, Alan A., *Dorking Gas Works,* DLHG Newsletter (New Series) 1, 1985.
65. Jackson, Alan A., *Dorking For Your Holidays and Health,* DLHG Newsletter (New Series) 1, 1985.
66. Jackson, Alan A., *Dorking's Railways,* DLHG, 1988.
67. Jackson, Alan A., (Ed), *Around Dorking in Old Photographs,* 1989.
68. Jackson, Alan A., *The Great By-Pass Controversy,* 'Dorking History' (DLHG), 4, 1990.
69. John, G, E., *Pixham Firs and Dorking in World War 2,* DLHG Newsletter (New Series), 5, 1987.
70. Keane, William, *The Beauties of Surrey: being a Particular Description of about 120 Seats of the Nobility and Gentry.....etc,* 1849.
71. Kidner, R, W., *The Reading to Tonbridge Line,* 1974.

72. Knight, David (Ed), *Dorking in Wartime,* 1989.

73. Kohler, Margaret, K, (Ed), *Memories of Old Dorking,* (recollections of Attlee, J, Dinnage R, and Rose, C), 1977.

74. Malden, H. E., *A History of Surrey,* 1900.

75. Manning, O, and Bray, W,. *The History and Antiquities of the County of Surrey,* vol 1, 1804.

76. [Mayo, Mary], *Pixham 1862–1912,* 1912.

77. [Mayo, Mary], *Concerning the Three Churches in Dorking dedicated to St. Martin, the Ancient, the Intermediate and the Present,* 1917.

78. Mercer, Doris *A Corner of West Street, Dorking: Six Centuries of Change,* DLHG, 1983.

79. Mercer, Doris, *The Deepdene, Dorking: Rise and Decline through Six Centuries,* SAC, vol 71, 1977.

80. Mercer, E. D., *The Dorking Brotherhood and Its Lands: and the Lands in Dorking of other Religious Bodies in the Tudor Period,* DLHG Newsletter (Old Series), 6, 1977.

81. Mercer, E. D., *The Dorking & Leith Hill District Preservation Society: Fifty Years of Conservation,* DLHG, 1980.

82. Mercer, Edith, and Mercer, Doris, *Henry Talbot of Chart Park, 1700–84,* 'Dorking History' (DLHG), 2, 1989.

83. Michell, A. R., *Surrey in 1649,* SAC, vol 67, 1970.

84. Mitchell, Vic, and Smith, Keith, *Southern Main Lines: Epsom to Horsham,* 1986.

85. Mitchell, Vic, and Smith, Keith, *Country Railway Routes: Guildford to Redhill,* 1989.

86. Miles, Lewis, *Guide to Dorking and District,* 1888.

87. Milne, F. A., (Ed), *Extracts from English Topography, Part XII, being part of a classified collection of the chief contents of 'The Gentleman's Magazine' from 1731 to 1868,* 1900.

88. Morris, John, *Domesday Book – Surrey,* 1975.

89. Morris, Joseph, *The Homeland Handbooks: Dorking, Leatherhead and Ashtead with their Surroundings,* 1918.

90. Mountford, Frances, *Nathaniel Wix, an 18th Century Dorking Worthy,* 'Dorking History' (DLHG) 3, 1990.

91. Nairn, Ian and Pevsner, Nikolaus, revised by Cherry, Bridget, *The Buildings of England: Surrey,* Second Edition 1971.

92. Newbury, Celia, (Ed), *Vaughan Williams in Dorking,* DLHG, 1979.

93. Newbury, Celia, (Ed), *A History of Sports in Dorking,* DLHG, 1985.

94. Overell, Brian, *The Medical Scene in Dorking in 1851,* DLHG Newsletter (New Series), 7, 1988.
95. Overell, Brian, *A Case of Blocked Drains,* DLHG Newsletter (New Series) 8, 1988.
96. Philpott, R. F., *St. Joseph's, Dorking. A Centenary History of the Church and Parish, 1872–1972,* 1972.
97. Scragg, R. S., *Three Hundred Years of Congregationalism in Dorking,* 1962.
98. Smail, H., *The Worthing Road and its Coaches,* 1944.
99. Smith, C. W., *Holmwood Notes,* DLHG Newsletter (Old Series), 15, 1982.
100. Stidder, D, *The Watermills of Surrey,* 1990.
101. Stiff, N. G. J., *The Church in Dorking and District,* 1912.
102. Sykes, Edwin, *Do Better Still, The Story of Powell Corderoy School (formerly The Dorking British School) 1816 to 1989,* DLHG, 1989.
103. Thompson, F. H., *Three Surrey Hillforts,* Antiquaries Journal, vol 59, 1979.
104. Thorne, W, *The Garden of Surrey, or a Sketch of Dorking and the Beautiful Country Surrounding It,* 1829.
105. Thorogood Irene, *Mary Alexander of Dorking (1741–1833),* DLHG Newsletter (New Series), 3, 1986.
106. Timbs, John, *A Picturesque Promenade round Dorking in Surrey,* 1823.
107. Townsend, Carole, *Our Cottage Hospitals,* 'Dorking History' (DLHG) 5, 1991.
108. Townsend, J. L., *Townsend Hook and the Railways of The Dorking Greystone Lime Co. Ltd.,* 1980.
109. Tucker, Brian (Ed), *And Choirs Singing: An Account of the Leith Hill Musical Festival 1905–85,* 1985.
110. Tyson, Dorothy, Ellen, *A Dorking Childhood,* 1979.
111. Vine, P. A. L., *London's Lost Route to the Sea,* 1973.
112. Walker, J. E. N., *An Old Dorking Family,* DHLG Newsletter, 8 (New Series), 1988.
113. Walker, T. E. C., *The White Horse Hotel, Dorking* SAC vol 54, 1955.
114. Wedgwood, Alexandra (Ed), *A History of the Church and Parish of St. Martin's, Dorking.* 1990.
115. Weight, Cliff, *The South Street Caves, Dorking,* DLHG, 1988.
116. Woolnough, J, *Pippbrook Mill and Dorking Memories,* DLHG Newsletter (New Series) 5, 6, 1987.

Unpublished papers and lectures:

117. Brigham, Allan, *Urban Growth in a Surrey Market Town: a Study of the Expansion of Dorking in the Mid-Nineteenth Century,* 1988.

118. Mercer, Edith, *The Battle of Dorking,* lecture to DLHG, 1988.

119. War Office Library, *A Note on the Surrey Defence Works of the Nineties and the circumstances of their Construction (with special reference to the works at Box Hill),* nd, c 1958 (Alan A Jackson Collection).

INDEX

nb: (1) All entries relate to Dorking unless otherwise noted.

(2) This index is also designed to be used by those seeking further reading; where relevant material is available, the page number in the bibliography (pp 110–116) is given, together with the number of the item in brackets to facilitate reference to the correct entry.

Abinger, ... 11, 67, 83
Agriculture, .. 12-13, 16, 21, 42, 55
Air, Qualities of the, ... 5, 6, 35
Air raids, ... 98, 99
Alexander, Mary, ... 61, 115 (105)
Almshouses, ...25, 26, 27, 32, 57, 59
Ambulance service, ... 101
American visitors, ... 69
Ankershagh, ... 14
Ansell Road, ... 75
Anstiebury, ... 11
Archery butts, ... 24
Archway Place, ... 45, 47, 93
Arthur, G. J. & Sons, ... 92
Arundel Road, ... 74, 116 (117)
Ashcombe/
Ashcombe Wood, ... 16,80
Ashcombe, Lord (1), ...77, 79-80, 85
Ashcombe, Lord (2), ... 98, 100
Ashcombe, Lord (3), ... 100
Ashcombe, Lord (4), ... 100
Ashcombe Road, ... 94, 99
Ashcombe School, ... 94
Assizes, ... 33
Attlee family/J. & W. Attlee, ...45 69, 88, 90, 111 (27)
Aubrey, John, ...5, 33, 35, 112 (29)
Back Lane, ... 9, 60, 61, 78
Band/Bandstand, ... 96
Baptists/Baptist Chapels, ... 78
Barclay family, ... 52, 83, 100 113 (62)
Barn Place 32
Bartlett family, ... 45, 114 (78)
Battle of Dorking, The, ... 85, 86, 98 112 (41), 116 (118)
Beetham-Wilson, J, ... 69, 111 (14)
Beresford Road, ... 92
Betchworth Castle,...21,23,29,33,51
Bevan, G. Phillips, ... 6, 79
Biwater, ... 100
Black Horse, The, ... 42
Bombs, ... 95, 99
Bonnets, ... 17
Borough English 17
Boxall's Brewery, ... 45
Box Hill, ... 32, 55, 68, 77, 85, 88, 116 (119)
Box, John, ... 85
Boys' High School, ... 83, 83-4
Bradley Estate/Bradley Farm ...13 21, 90
Brethren, The, ... 78
Brewing/Breweries, ... 26, 45, 87
Brickmaking, ... 33, 67, 87
Bright, J. S., ...6, 112 (39), 113 (53)
British School, ...61, 84, 85, 112 (45) 115 (102)
Broad, William, ... 47
Broadwood, James, ... 57
Brockham, ... 43, 103
Brookes, William McIntosh, ... 76
Brookside, ... 47
Brotherhood, – *see* Fraternity
Browne family, .. 23, 25, 26, 29, 31 32, 33, 57, 59, 113 (62)
Bull's Head, The, ... 47
Burchet House School, ... 85
Burrell, Sir William, ... 49
Bury Hill, ... 52, 83, 100 113 (70)

Bus Garage, ... 97-8
Bush Inn, The, ... 40
Business Park, ... 107
Bus services,...88, 93, 97-8, 112 (31)
Butter Hill, .. 15, 16, 23, 61, 71, 78
Butter Hill House, ... 54
By-pass – *see* Deepdene Avenue
Calvert Road, ... 94, 99
Canals, ... 38, 115 (111)
Candle factories, ... 67
Canterbury Court, ... 107
Capel, ... 15, 17, 67, 83
Cardinal's Hat, The, ... 16
Cars – *see* Motor Traffic
Castle Mill, ... 23, 87
Caves, ... 34, 35, 115 (115)
Cemetery, ... 79
Chadhurst Farm, ... 52
Chalcraft, A, ... 69
Chalkpit Lane, ... 42, 102
Chance, Maurice, ...90, 102, 113 (63)
Charities, ... 27, 59-60
Chart Downs, ... 17, 93
Chart Lane, ... 17, 43
Chart Lane Institute, ... 84, 85, 94
Chart Park, ... 17, 50, 51, 114 (82)
Cheesman's Brewery, ... 45
Chequers, The, ... 26, 27
Chequers Place, ... 93
Chergate/Chertgate Lane, ... 9
Chert, ... 17
Chert, John atte, ... 13
Chichester,
Canon Edward, Arthur, ... 7
Chichester Road, ... 94, 99
Chippingburgh, ... 15
Christian Centre, ... 78
Churches, Parish, ... 12, 19, 20, 21, 25, 31, 60, 76-7, 78, 79, 114 (77) 115 (101), 115, (114)
Church Gardens, ... 93
Churchill, Winston 79
Church Street, ... 9, 11, 45, 60, 61, 78, 93
Churchwardens, ... 25
Cinema Royal, ... 104
Cinemas, ... 104-5
Civil War, ... 29
Clarendon House, ... 54, 84
Clear, A. & P. 92
Clift, Joseph, ... 75
Cliftonville 75
Climate, ... 5, 6
Club Court, ... 104
Clutton, H, ... 79
Coaches, road, ... 47-8, 68, 69, 115 (98)
Coal trade, ... 43
Coast Hill, ... 40
Cock, Dorking – *see* Fowl
Cock Inn, The, ... 39
Coldharbour, ... 67, 83
Coldharbour Lane,...9, 33, 37, 74, 78
Commons (*see also* Cotmandene, Holmwood, Spital Heath),...13, 33
Congregationalism/Church, ... 32, 61, 78, 113 (55), 115 (97)
Conservation Areas, ... 96
Corderoy, Miss E. M., ... 84
Corn trade,...42, 45, 69, 71, 88, 90, 111 (27), 115 (116)
Cosens, Samuel, ... 31, 32
Cotmandene, ... 5, 12, 26, 33, 35, 51, 54, 59, 62, 68, 71, 75, 83, 93
Cottage Hospital, – *see* Hospitals
Councils – *see* Mole Valley, Urban District Council
Council housing/estates, ... 92-93
County School, ... 94
County Secondary Modern Mixed School, ... 94
Court Close, ... 17
Crawford, William, ... 75
Cricket, ... 62, 112 (43)
Crime – *see* Law and Order
Cross House, ... 14
Croucher & Co., Herbert 69
Crow, Messrs/Crow F. Lewis,...69, 71
Cubitt, George *see* Ashcombe, Lord (1)
Cubitt, Thomas, ... 79, 113 (61) 113 (62)
Culpin, Clifford, ... 93
Cummins & Sons, ... 69

Davis, A. F., ... 102
Dawson, The Rev. Alfred, ... 61
Deepdene Avenue (By-pass), ...90
95-96, 99, 113 (68)
Deepdene, The, mansions, gardens, park and estate 5, 33, 48-51
79, 90, 96, 99, 113 (70), 114 (79)
Deepdene Gardens, ... 51
Deepdene Park Estate, ... 90
113 (63)
Deepdene Vale, ... 90
Defoe, Daniel, . 5, 31, 32, 37, 42, 50
112 (30), 112 (46), 113 (62)
Degenhardt, Charles, ... 88
Denbies, ... 51, 79-80, 90, 98, 99
100, 102, 113 (61), 113 (70)
Dendy, Arthur, ... 74
Dene, John and Odo atte, ... 17
Dene Street,...9, 24, 33, 54, 88, 93
Denison, Joseph, ... 51
Denison, William Joseph, ... 51, 79
113 (62)
Dennis, John, ... 9, 112 (47)
Disraeli, Benjamin, ... 79
Dissenters, ... 32-33, 60
Domesday/Domesday era, ... 12-13
113 (51), 114 (88)
Dorking Brick Company, ... 67
87, 92
Dorking Gas Company,...80, 101
113 (64)
Dorking Gas Light Company, .. 80
113 (64)
Dorking Halls, ... 104, 105
Dorking Villa Building Company, ... 74
Dorking Water Company 70
80-1, 101
Douglas, Miss F. M, ... 7
Down, Scott & Down, ... 69
Downs Lane, ... 9
Drainage – *see* Sewerage
Drill hall, ... 85
Driver, Charles H., ... 73, 83
Dudley House, ... 84
Dutch House, ... 53-54
Eastburgh, ... 15
East Street, ... 9
East Surrey Gas Company, ... 101
East Surrey Traction Company, ... 97, 112 (31)
East Surrey Water Company, .. 101
Ebenezer Row, ... 78
Effingham, ... 58
Electricity supply/works, ... 100-1
Embassy, The, ... 104
Evacuees, ... 98, 99
Evelyn, family, ... 5, 84, 113 (62)
Evening Classes, ... 85
Fair, annual, ... 15, 35, 42, 71
Fairfield Drive, ... 102
Falkland Road/Falkland District, ... 74, 75, 78, 84, 93
116 (117)
Farms/Farming – *see* Agriculture and specific names of farms,
Feake, Christopher, ... 32
Federated House, ... 106
Ferrey, Benjamin, ... 77
Fire Brigade/Stations 83, 101
Firestone quarry, ... 67
Fisher, James, ... 32
Foe, James, ... 31
Football Club/Ground, ... 24, 102
114 (93)
Football, Shrove Tuesday, ...62
114 (93)
Foreignburgh, ... 15
Forestry Corps, ... 98
Forman, William Henry, ... 75
Forster, William, ... 31
Forts, ... 85, 116 (119)
Foundlings, nursing of, ... 45
Fowl, Dorking,...35, 42, 102 112 (33)
Fox & Hounds Inn, The, ... 39
Frampton, E. Reginald, ... 98
Fraser, Sir Malcolm & Lady, ... 92
Fraser Gardens, ... 92, 93, 99
Fraternity of The Blessed Mary, (Brotherhood), ... 20, 21
25, 26, 114 (80)

Friends, *see* Society of Friends
Friends' Provident and Century
Assurance offices, ... 105
Fuller family and shops, ... 69, 86
Gallows, ... 33, 37
Gardens, gardening, ... 33, 48, 49
79, 99
Gas supply/works, ... 80, 101, 107
113 (64)
Geology, ... 11, 35, 37
Geography, ... 11
George, The 16
Gettings, S. S., ... 92
Giles Green, ... 39, 58
Girls' High School, ... 84, 107
111 (12)
Glory, The, ... 11, 92
Goodwyn family, ... 23, 26
Goodwyns (Goodwins)
Farm/Estate, ... 15, 93, 94
Goodwyns Place, ... 76
Gospel Hall, ... 78
Green Line Coaches, ... 98
Guardians, Board of, ... 58
Guild, /Guild House 21
Guildford, ... 38, 57
Gun, The, ... 107, 114 (78)
Haggle van service, ... 48
Hampstead Lane, ... 13
Hampstead Road, ... 40, 74,78
93, 116 (117)
Hamsted, ... 13
Harrow Gate, ... 40
Harrow Road, ... 74, 116 (117)
Hart, John/Hart,
Scales & Hodges, ... 69
Hart Road, ... 75, 78
Health resort – *see* Invalids
Hearth Tax, ... 33, 111 (21)
Henn, William, ... 23
Henry III, ... 14
High Street, ... 9, 16, 21, 23, 27
31, 34, 35, 39, 42, 45, 47, 53-4, 54
68, 69, 70, 71, 82, 88, 95, 96, 97, 102
104, 107
High Street Buildings, ... 70, 78
History, lack of, ... 9
Holidays/Holiday resort, ...5, 6, 63
68-9, 75, 88, 113 (65)
Holloway Estate/Farm, ... 6, 15, 75
Hollows, The, ... 39, 40
Holmwood, ... 11, 12-13, 15, 16
24, 33, 38, 40, 67, 87, 92, 101, 103,
115 (99)
Homewood - *see* Holmwood
Hope, Henry Thomas, ... 50
113 (62), 114 (79)
Hope. Mrs. A. A. 81, 114 (79)
Hope, Thomas, ... 49, 50
113 (62), 114 (79)
Horsham Road 11, 40, 59, 60
74, 75, 93, 97, 116 (117)
Hospitals, ... 80, 81, 92
94-5, 111 (13), 115 (107)
Housebuilding – *see* Residential
growth,
Howard, family, ... 25, 31, 61-2,
113 (62)
Howard, Charles, ...5, 33, 48, 50, 59
Howard, Charles, Jr, ... 48
Howard, Henry, ... 31, 50
Howard, Henry Charles, ... 48
Howard Road, ... 74, 116 (117)
Industries 16, 33, 42-6, 45
67, 87, 92
Inhabitants – *see* People, Population
Inner Relief Road Scheme, ... 96
Innes, Michael 103
Inns (*see also specific names*) ... 16
26-27, 35, 40, 63, 70-1, 107
Invalids recuperating
at Dorking, ... 54, 63, 113 (65)
Iron Foundry, ... 45, 87, 114, (78)
Isolation Hospital, ... 94-5
Ivery & Son, James, ... 69
Ivy Holt, ... 84
Jennings, Louis, J, ... 5-6, 71
Jubilee Terrace, ... 75, 84
Keppel Road, ... 19, 99, 100
Kingham, H. G & Co., ... 88, 107
King's Arms, The,...26, 32, 114 (78)
King's Head, The, ... 27, 45, 47
48, 63, 64, 82, 83

Knoll Road, ... 75
Labelliere, Peter, ... 54
Law and Order, ... 16-17, 19, 33
55, 57, 78, 83
Lear, Edward, ... 42
Leith Hill Musical Competitions/
Festivals, ... 105, 115 (109)
Leslie family, ... 52-3
Library, ... 103
Limemaking, ... 42-3, 87
Lincoln Road, ... 75, 93
Little Dudley House, ... 33, 34, 84
Local Board of Health, .. 71, 81, 82
Local government, *see* Local Board of Health,
Mole Valley District Council,
Rural Sanitary District, Union,
Urban District Council, Vestry.
Local History Group, ... 100
Londesbrough, Lord, ... 79
London Road, ... 9, 23, 24, 39
69, 75, 84, 102
Longfield Road, ... 94
Lonsdale Road, ... 75
Louis Philippe,
King of France, ... 54
Lower Chequers, The, ... 26
Lucock's Brewery, ... 45
Lutyens, Edwin, ... 78
Lyon's Court, ... 93
Mc Lennan, Jim, ... 7
McMorran, Donald H, ... 93
Magazine Society, ... 63
Magistrates – *see* Law and Order
Magistrates' Courts, ... 70, 83, 107
Manor, ... 12, 13, 15-21
23, 31, 33, 38, 48, 49, 71
Manor courts, ... 17-18, 19, 33
110 (6) (7)
Market, ... 15, 16, 23, 35, 40
42, 69, 71, 87, 90, 96, 111 (9)
Market House, ... 23, 33, 38
Marlborough, Lily,
Duchess of, ... 79, 82, 114 (79)
Marlborough Road, ... 92
Marsh, Lawrence, ... 31, 32, 52
Martineau, Howard, ... 76, 93
105, 113 (62)
Mason, Joseph, ... 69
Meadowbank, ... 24, 102
Meredith, George, ... 77, 113 (62)
Meredith, Percy W, ... 105
Methodism/Methodist
Churches, ... 61, 78, 112 (38)
Mickleham, ... 21, 67, 83, 103
Mill Lane, ... 17, 23, 43, 44
45, 93, 101
Millpond, ... 102
Mills, ... 12, 16, 23, 24, 45
87, 113 (60), 115 (100), 115 (116)
Milton Court, ... 45, 99
Milton/Milton Heath, ... 11, 15, 23
Mineral water works, ... 67, 90
Mole, River, ... 11, 16, 38
Mole Valley
District Council, ... 103, 112 (28)
Moore, James 84
Moore's Road, ... 83, 84
Motor Traffic, ... 86, 92, 95-8
Mowbray County Secondary
Modern School, ... 94
Mullins, William,... 26, 28, 113 (62)
Murders, ... 14
Museum, ... 100
Name, ... 12, 111 (19)
National Freehold
Land Society, ... 74, 116 (117)
National School, ... 84
Newcastle, Duke of, ... 92, 105
Newdigate, ... 67
New Electric Cinema, ... 104
Newman, Robert, ... 33
Nonconformism, *see* Baptists,
Congregationalism, Dissenters,
Methodism.
Norfolk, Dukes of, ... 38, 48, 49
61-2, 71, 78, 83
North Holmwood *see* Holmwood
North Street, ... 9, 26, 60, 93
114 (78)
Nower, The, ... 83

Nower Road, ... 92
Nurseries, nurserymen, .. 33, 69, 75
Ockley, ... 67, 83
Oddfellows' Hall, ... 70
Odo, Bishop of Bayeux, ... 13
Offices, ... 90, 99, 105-7
Olivier, Gerard, ... 85
One Way System, ... 96-7
Orchard Road, ... 93
Page, William, ... 52
Parkway, ... 102
Parsonage lands, ... 20, 25
Parsonage House, ... 84, 107
Parsonage Mill, ... 45, 69, 87, 107
Patching Mill *see* Pippbrook Mill
Patching, Resta,
Jr. and Sr, ... 47, 54, 113 (62)
Pavilion, The 104
Pierson, C. J. & Co., ... 69
People, ... 7, 31, 35, 113 (62)
Philps family, ... 63, 113 (62)
Pilgrim Fathers, ... 26
Pipes, clay 44
Pipes, water, ... 43-4
Pip Lane, ... 9
Pippbrook, The, ... 45, 47, 81
Pippbrook Council Offices, ... 103
Pippbrook mansion, ... 52, 75-6
90, 102-3
Pippbrook Mill, ... 23, 24, 45
81, 87, 102, 115 (116)
Pixham, ... 23, 53, 77-8, 81
82, 103, 105, 114 (76)
Pixham Church, ... 77-8, 114
(76), 115 (101)
Pixham End, ... 105
Pixham Lane, ... 9
Pixham Mill, ... 23, 45. 81, 87
Pixham School, ... 84, 114 (76)
Plagues, ... 21, 29, 33
Playhouse, The, ... 105
Police/Police Stations, ... 55, 83
95, 107
Poor, relief of the /Poverty
see also Almshouses, Charities,
Workhouses, ... 25-6, 27, 55
57-60, 71, 78
Population, ... 9, 12, 23, 33, 37
64, 73, 87, 92, 103, 109
Postal and telegraph services and post
offices, ... 47, 67, 82-3
Potteries, ... 43-4
Poultry, ... 35, 42
Powell, T. E, ... 76, 84
Powell Corderoy School, ... 84, 94
112 (45), 115 (102)
Prehistoric settlements, ... 11
Preservation Society, ... 99, 100
106, 114 (81)
Preston, F. Leslie & Easton,
John M, ... 105
Priests, ... 20, 25, 31, 32, 51
Priory of The Holy Cross, ... 20
Priory Convent School, ... 84
Public Hall, ... 83, 84, 101, 105
Pump/Pump Corner, ... 15, 16, 47
Punchbowl Inn, ... 106
Punishments, ... 19, 33
Puritan sympathies/
puritanism, ... 26, 29, 31, 32
Quakers – *see* Society of Friends
Quarter sessions, ... 33, 111 (23)
Queen's Arms, ... 26, 45, 114 (78)
Queen's Head, ... 39, 40
Railways, ... 11, 68, 69, 71
72, 73, 88, 90, 98, 112 (44), 113 (56)
113 (66), 113 (71), 114 (84) (85)
Railway stations, ... 69, 71, 73
88, 90,113 (56), 113 (66)
Ram Alley, ... 9, 24
Ram Inn, ... 106
Ranmore, ... 57, 67, 77, 85
116 (118)
Reading, Guildford & Reigate
Railway Company ...71, 112 (44)
Recluse, ... 14
Red Lion Brewery, ... 45
Red Lion, The, ... 16, 42, 45, 55
57, 63, 64, 70-1, 97, 107
Refugees (from London), ... 98
Refugees (from Europe), ... 99
Refuse/Refuse Disposal, ... 82, 87
Regent,The, ... 104

Reigate Castle, ... 13, 14, 16, 17
Reigate Road, ... 37, 79, 101, 106
Residential growth, ... 48, 73-5, 90, 92-3, 99-100, 102, 111 (10), 113 (63) 116 (117)
Retail trade – *see* Shops
Retirement, ... 5, 6
Richard of Clare, ... 13
Ridgeway Road, ... 33, 75
Riots, 1830, ... 55-7
Roads, *(see also* specific names) 5, 11, 12 35, 37–40, 47–8, 82, 95, 96, 113 (68)
Roman Catholics, (*see* also St. Joseph's) 33, 61-2, 78 84, 115 (96)
Roman era, ... 5, 9, 11
Roman Road, ... 75
Ropemakers' walk, ... 40
Rose Hill, ... 54, 68, 74, 85 102, 116 (117)
Rothes, Earl of, ... 53
Rothes Road, ... 53, 75
Rowe, Charles J, ... 69
Royal Electric, The, ... 104
Royal Oak, The, ... 52, 53
Rural Sanitary Authority/District, ... 67, 81
Ryder, William, ... 93
St. Barnabas Church (Ranmore), ... 77, 98, 115 (101)
St. Joseph's Church, ...78, 115 (96)
St. Joseph's School, ... 78, 84 115 (96)
St. Martin (dedication), *see also* Churches, Parish). 21
St. Martin's First and Middle Schools, ... 84, 94
St. Martin's (C of E) High School – *see* Girls' High School
St. Martin's Walk, ... 90, 108
St. Paul's Church, ... 77, 115 (101)
St. Paul's Road, ... 60, 75, 85
St. Paul's School, ... 84
Sackville, William, ... 23
Salvation Army, ... 6, 78, 104
Sandy Cross, ... 9, 33
Sandy Cross Lane, ... 9
Sandy Lane, ... 9
Sanitation, ... 81–2, 115 (95)
Saxons, ... 12
Scenery, ... 5, 6
Schools (*see also* names of specific schools), ... 32, 60 61, 83-5, 94
Scott, Sir George Gilbert, ... 76, 77
Sewerage Schemes/ Sewage Works, ... 81, 82 103, 115 (95)
Shearburn, William Sr, ... 59, 61 113 (62)
Shearburn, William Jr, ... 70, 82 113 (62)
Shearburn, William Joseph, ... 73 113 (62)
Sheridan, Richard Brinsley, ... 49
Sherlock & Son, T. H., ... 69
Shops/ Shopkeepers, ... 23, 24 69-70, 75, 88, 90
Shrub Hill, ... 31, 52 53, 66, 75
Sims, George R, ... 6
Site, ... 11
Slum Housing and demolition, ... 64, 75, 82, 93
Smallpox, ... 44
Smith, Henry, ... 27, 60
Social life, ... 5-6
Society of Friends/ Meeting House, ... 60,78
Solicitors, ... 69, 112 (40)
Sondes family, ... 21, 23
Sondes Place, ... 60
Sondes Place Farm, ... 21
Sondes Place School, ... 94
Southern Railway Company, ... 99
South Street, ... 15, 26, 33 34, 35, 39, 45, 47, 54, 57, 58, 59, 60 68, 69, 71, 78, 82, 83, 85, 88, 96, 97 98, 104, 106, 113 (54), 113 (58)
South Terrace, ... 74, 81, 85 92, 116 (117)
Sparrow Club, ... 35

Spital Heath, ... 71
Spratley, Robert, ... 69
Spring Gardens, ... 32, 54, 93
Stage coaches *see* Coaches, road
Stane Street, ... 5, 11, 12, 37
Stanway School, ... 94
Station Road, ... 9, 67, 69, 80, 82
83, 84, 101, 107
Stone & Turner, ...45, 88, 114 (78)
Stoneleigh, ... 7
Streets – *see* Roads and specific names,
Strood Lane, ... 9
Surrey Yeoman, The, ... 53
Swimming Baths/Centre, ... 83, 101
Talbot, Henry, ... 50, 114, (82)
Tannery, ... 16, 44
Taylor & Brooker, ... 67, 101
Telephone Exchanges/
Service, ... 101-2
Tennis, ... 24
Theatricals, ... 63, 71, 83
Thorne, James, ... 5
Thorne, W, ... 5, 115 (104)
Thornton, George, ... 44, 113 (59)
Three Tuns, The, ... 42, 71, 96
Timber cutting and trade, ... 15
16, 35, 38, 67, 98, 101
Timbs, John, ...5, 63, 64, 115 (106)
Tithes, tithe barn, ... 20, 51
Tollbars/Tollgates, ... 39, 40
Tourist trade – *see* Holidays
Tower Hill/Tower Hill Road, ... 24
74, 75, 76, 80, 85, 92, 116 (117)
Town Improvement
Association, ... 75
Town Mill, ... 23, 24
Town Planning Scheme (1939),...92
Tracks – *see* Roads,
Trippers, ... 68, 88, 90, 97
Turner, H. Thackeray, ... 76
Turnpike Roads/
Turnpike Trust,...39-40, 47, 70, 81
Tyers, Jonathan, ... 51, 113 (62)
Union/Union Workhouse, ... 58-9
67, 78, 94, 113 (50)
Urban District Council, ... 82, 87
92-3, 101, 102, 103, 105
Vaughan Williams, Ralph, ... 105
113 (62), 114 (92), 115 (109)
Vestry, the, ... 25, 27, 33, 44, 47, 81
Vicarages, ... 33, 60, 77
Vicars – *see* Priests,
Vincent ('s) Lane,...30, 60, 97, 107
Vineyards, ... 50, 100
Vintage House, ... 50
Volunteers, ... 85
Waldburgh, ... 15
Walker family, ... 47, 48, 115 (112)
Walter, Edward, ... 52
Warenne family, ...13, 14, 15, 20, 21
Warrener, the lord's, ... 19
Wars – *see* World War
Watermills – *see* Mills
Water souchy, ... 63-4
Waterworks, ... 45, 47, 80-1, 101
Wathen, Augustus, ... 53
Wathen Road, ... 53, 69, 75
Wesley, John 61
Westcott, ... 15, 32, 45
67, 93, 95, 103
Westhumble, ... 67, 103
Weston, Harry, ... 104
West Street, ... 15, 16, 26
28, 40, 44, 45, 54, 61, 62, 68, 78, 83,
84, 88, 96, 97, 114 (78)
Wheatsheaf, The, ... 35, 63, 107
White, Adrian, ... 100
White & Sons, ... 69, 71
White Horse, The, ... 14, 35, 48
54, 68, 69, 115 (113)
Windmill, ... 23-4
Windmill Inn, ... 40
Woodyer, Henry, ... 77
Workhouses, ... 26, 57-9, 74, 78, 94
113 (50), 114 (90)
World War I, ... 96, 98, 111 (14)
World War II, ... 95, 96, 98-9
113 (69), 114 (72)
Wornum, G. Grey, ... 92
Wotton, ... 53, 55
Yew Tree Road, ... 99
Young's Brewery, ... 45